Making Change Happen by Jane Northcote has been enthusiastically received by business people from large organisations and small businesses, by Jane's fellow consultants, and by academics in the field of change. Here's what they say:

'In *Making Change Happen* Jane makes implementing change both easy and accessible. She distils management consulting methodologies into simple and powerful truths. Uplifting, inspirational and exciting – this is the "start here" button for anyone involved in business change. Change is possible, you can do it, today, and here's how.'

- *Robert Smithbury, consultant and business owner, Precise Business Services*

'This book has taught me the difference between action and activity. I have learned that things only get done by taking direct action, and that sometimes it is too easy just to be active. Since reading this book, I find myself questioning "Is this action or just activity?" I ask it of myself and my managers, and I never leave a meeting without everyone being clear on what has to be done to make things happen. Like all the best things, this is surprisingly simple, but it has made a big difference to my company.'

- *Nigel Phillipps, managing director, Unity Information Systems*

'A book you'll wish you'd read before you last tried to make a change happen in your organisation – and will want to revisit before you try again.'

- *Jonathan Harker, founding director, Catalise plc*

'I really enjoyed this book. Having read business books in the past which are full of jargon, I found Jane's book interesting to read, full of energy and aesthetically beautiful, with Lizzie Everard's illustrations really bringing the content to life. *Making Change Happen* prompts the reader to reappraise the opportunities that arise.'

- *Karen Napier, Director of Development, Southbank Centre*

‘Although this book can be read in about an hour, you’ll want to read it again and again. Its messages are clear and practical, because this is a book that is based on experience, tempered with reflection and insight.’

- *Dr Janet Smart, Director, BT Centre for Major Programme Management, Said Business School, University of Oxford*

‘This book has immense practical application for all businesses. There are disciplines in it that will fundamentally improve organisational performance. Down to earth, straightforward and practical, Jane writes in a way that is both modest and highly compelling – a rare combination.’

- *Nick Bush, consultant*

‘This book deals with change, focusing right where the action is – the conversations and interactions between people. Clear, punchy messages are brought to life with workplace scenarios we all recognise, and are written with an energy and verve that make these messages truly memorable.’

- *Rebecca Wallace, independent learning and development consultant*

MAKING CHANGE HAPPEN

IMPLEMENTING BUSINESS CHANGE

• *a practical guide* •

Jane Northcote

JN

First published in the United Kingdom in 2008 by

Jane Northcote
162 Cromwell Tower, Barbican
London EC2Y 8DD

www.JaneNorthcote.com

First issued in a limited edition of 1000 copies in February 2008

A copy of the British Library Cataloguing in Publication data is available from the British Library

ISBN-13: 978-0-9557760-0-7

Project managed and produced by Sonja Jefferson, www.sonjajefferson.com

Editorial consultant: Paul Forty at Brookes Forty, www.brookesforty.com

Website consultancy and design: Ian Head at Head-E Design Ltd, www.head-e.com

Typeset in Univers Condensed and Baskerville

Printed and bound in Italy by Legoprint S.p.A., Lavis, Trento

To John

WHAT IF THIS ROAD

What if this road, that has held no surprises
these many years, decided not to go
home after all; what if it could turn
left or right with no more ado
than a kite-tail? What if its tarry skin
were like a long, supple bolt of cloth,
that is shaken and rolled out, and takes
a new shape from the contours beneath?
And if it chose to lay itself down
in a new way; around a blind corner,
across hills you must climb without knowing
what's on the other side; who would not hanker
to be going, at all risks? Who wants to know
a story's end, or where a road will go?

• *Sheenagh Pugh* *note 1*

CONTENTS

	Introduction	1
1	Making change happen	7
2	Declare your intention	13
3	Describe the change	31
4	Choose effective action	57
5	Get into action	73
6	Be aware	85
7	Continue	97
8	Conversations that work	111
9	Meetings where change happens	123
	Conclusion	133
	Notes	140
	Index	146
	Acknowledgements	150

INTRODUCTION

This is a book about getting things done in organisations. As a consultant I discover that lots of people have ideas about how to improve things. My interest is in getting those ideas implemented: making change happen.

I am a management consultant: my work is to accelerate action. My clients are leaders who want to get something done. They've emerged from an inspirational corporate event, or they've just completed a strategy study. They've identified a problem to be tackled or an opportunity to be seized. They are faced with an employee survey which demands action, or they've got some customer feedback they can't ignore. They sit at their desk on Monday morning with the large lever-arch file at their elbow. They look out across the open-plan office and they ask themselves: 'What now?' It is for them, and for you, that this book is written.

My aim in this book was to collect together in a coherent way the principles that I use in my work. I wanted to create a book with pictures and conversations, as an alternative to the many business books that are thick with text. The business world is alive with images and dialogue, and I am keen to convey that spirit and liveliness.

I've concentrated on the implementation stage of projects: the part where action happens. It is the difficult bit, and, in my view, the interesting bit. *note 2*
It is the stage which delivers a result.

Before the implementation, there may be strategic thinking, analysis and much planning. When the framework has been presented, the analysis

WHAT NOW?

completed, the strategy decided and the plan established, then somebody has to do something. This book is for that moment.

Many change methodologies describe change at the level of the corporation: strategic change or transformative change. They focus on planning. I am interested in change from the point of view of the individuals who are working inside the organisation at departmental, functional or team level. I focus on action. The methods and principles I describe in this book are from this viewpoint. *note 3*

Making large changes happen is about making many small local changes. Each small local change is an effort and an accomplishment. This, for me, is the importance and excitement of implementation: people achieve something, their world changes and the potential effect is far-reaching.

The purpose of this book is to help you structure your thoughts and take decisive action to make the change you want in your organisation. It will help you distinguish action, which is what makes change happen, from other activities which do not. It offers you specific techniques for getting into action and making progress.

The stories and examples I've used are from my clients and from people I have interviewed specifically for this book. All the stories are true. I have not invented anything, although sometimes I have formed a composite story from recurring patterns I have observed. Where people have agreed, I have used their names and given their contact details. In other cases I have changed the names and details of the story to protect the privacy of the protagonists.

This book sets out what has worked for me. The margins of the pages are wide, so that you can add your own comments and write in the book.

If you agree, or disagree, with anything I've written here, and you'd like to tell me, please email me. If you have a good story, an example, or a counter-example, then I'm keen to hear from you. You can communicate with me either by email: *jane@JaneNorthcote.com* or via my website: *www.JaneNorthcote.com.* The website also has more examples, further ideas, links and chapters of future books.

HERE IS A PLAN OF THE BOOK . . .

DEFINITIONS
- *Chapter 1: Making change happen*

BASIC PRINCIPLES
- *Chapter 2: Declare your intention* →
- *Chapter 3: Describe the change* →
- *Chapter 4: Choose effective action* →
- *Chapter 5: Get into action* →
- *Chapter 6: Be aware* →
- *Chapter 7: Continue* →

TECHNIQUES
- *Chapter 8: Conversations that work*
- *Chapter 9: Meetings where change happens*

FINAL THOUGHTS & SUMMARY
- *Conclusion*

note 4 Chapters 2–7 form a step-by-step method. There are many other such methods and some are listed in the notes. The notes for all chapters are at the end of the book.

. . . AND A BASIC METHOD FOR ACTION-ORIENTED CHANGE

STEP 1 *Declare your intention*

WHAT AM I TRYING TO ACHIEVE?

State what you are trying to achieve.
Say it clearly, so people hear.

STEP 2 *Describe the change you want in terms of from and to*

WHAT DIFFERENCE WILL IT MAKE?

Ask people, especially those affected by the change, what's needed to make it happen.
Work out what's going to be different, and what's going to stay the same.

STEP 3 *Choose effective action*

WHAT SHALL I DO?

Do the things which have an effect, not the things which have no effect.
Do the things which have the biggest effect and the greatest chance of success.
Do the things which most directly deliver the outcome.

STEP 4 *Get into action*

DO IT!

Take action.
Do it now.

STEP 5 *Be aware*

WHAT'S HAPPENING?

Be attentive while in action.
Participate in what you are creating.

STEP 6 *Continue*

WHAT'S NEXT?

Be influenced by the effects of your action.
Revise or restate your intention. Get into action again.

1 MAKING CHANGE HAPPEN

The messages in this chapter are:

- 'making change happen' means 'turning intention into reality'
- small changes make a difference

WHY MAKE CHANGE HAPPEN?

In business, things are changing around us all the time. You walk into work, sit at your desk, and you are confronted by all sorts of changes happening. In just one week, for example, in a headquarters department of a high street bank, an operations manager was dealing with the following changes:

- Five of my colleagues, systems management people, have been transferred to an outsourcer. I don't know if I can still ask them to perform the data scans they used to do for me.
- Group IT is upgrading some, but not all, of the equipment I use. I must co-ordinate my work schedules with them.
- These young people we've recruited are sending each other instant messages during our audio conference calls. I should probably find out from them how to do this messaging, and join in.
- New regulations mean that I must complete these assessments as part of our corporate risk management policy. I have to sign as 'Accountable Executive' and I'm not entirely sure I know what that implies in this case.

- My operations team is testing some data back-up procedures to eliminate the problem we had at last month-end. It seems to be taking them rather a long time, and we are nearly at month-end again.

Like this manager, anyone in business is already engaged with the changes that are arriving unbidden on their desk. Change happens to us and around us without our having to do anything. So why do we want to make it happen?

We want to make change happen because we want to have things turn out the way WE intend. We want to be doing it, not having it done to us. We have an idea how things could be better, and we intend to do something about it. We want to have an effect, to make a difference. We want to be the agents of change and not the victims of it.

This is what I mean by *making change happen.*

MAKING change happen — *Having things turn out the way you intend*

making CHANGE happen — *Having things turn out differently from how they would have done without your intervention* / *Having things turn out differently from how they were before*

making change HAPPEN — *Implementing the change – taking action which makes a difference*

When we say **MAKING**, we imply that you are taking the initiative. You might be the originator of the change, or you might be carrying forward an element of a wider programme. In both cases, to carry the initiative you need to be clear what you want, as we will see in Chapter 2.

When we say **CHANGE**, we mean that things will be different afterwards. Specifying this difference is an important skill, which we shall consider in Chapter 3.

When we say **HAPPEN**, we mean that the change will be implemented. This is the serious business of taking action, described in Chapters 4, 5, 6 and 7.

SMALL CHANGES ARE SIGNIFICANT

Many small changes add up to a big change. The great business transformations are achieved by many people taking individual actions in their immediate environment. For example, integrating the operations of two great corporations is achieved by many adjustments in procedure, roles, incentives and loyalties. It is in the minutiae of day-to-day life in the workplace that change is accomplished. A 'step-change' in customer service or product profitability happens when a large number of people take individual actions in their areas, some of which are very remote from customers or products.

Often these local actions seem straightforward. Often, all we would like to see is that every stock item is correctly entered in the asset database, or that all project managers have received PRINCE2 training. We want to know that the finance systems are correct and that the three databases containing finance information are consistent with one another. These sound like simple things.

Yet getting simple things done in organisations is far from straightforward. Anyone who has implemented a business transformation knows the importance, and difficulty, of consistent action at the working level.

These small operational changes are sometimes lost in the large-scale approaches to change. But they are not just details. It is these small actions which make the difference. *note 5*

The examples in this book describe such small local changes.

MANY SMALL CHANGES ADD UP TO A

BIG
CHANGE
TINY
detail
function
INDIVIDUAL
ELEMENT
ADJUSTMENTS
LOCAL
SIMPLE THINGS
COMPONENT
IMMEDIATE
ITEM
small
NOW
minutiae
CONSISTENT ACTION
INTENTION
SMALL
DETAIL
specific
CONSISTENT
SIMPLE
element
large number
LEVEL
DIFFERENCE
things
FUNCTION
WORKING LEVEL

2 DECLARE YOUR INTENTION

What am I trying to achieve?

The previous chapter explained that this book is about making things happen: that is – having things turn out as you intend. So we first make sure you can state your intention: 'What am I trying to achieve?' That is the question for this chapter. The rest of the book addresses how to make that intention become reality.

The messages in this chapter are:

- Be sure you have an intention. At all times be ready to answer the question 'What am I trying to achieve?'
- Intention is not vision, intention is your direction now
- Declare your intention: say what you are trying to do and say what you are not trying to do

WHAT IS YOUR INTENTION HERE?

It's very easy to get caught up in daily activity and lose track of what we are trying to achieve. Then we waste time being 'unproductive' because we haven't worked out in which direction we are trying to go. Intentions need not be lofty or visionary, but unless we have an intention we are the receivers of change rather than the instigators of it.

Here follow some ways in which people have described their intentions to me. They are all personal statements, driving individual people's action. They are answers to the question 'What are you trying to achieve?'

'I want to show that I can make the transition from being a civil servant to being a successful manager in the private sector.'

'I want to get my bonus, then get out of here.'

'I am getting this place properly organised. That means I must make the operations run smoothly so I can concentrate on strategy, which is what really interests me.'

'I want to do a good job. I always do a good job. In this case the job I've been given is to roll out the corporate intranet to our subsidiaries. I intend to do it, and I intend to do it well.'

'I am demonstrating to the Board that there really is a profitable business here.'

Each of the examples opposite is a real example from someone I have known. In each case, the statement they made was driving their decisions and their actions on a daily basis.

What are you trying to achieve, now, at this moment? This is an essential question, and not always easy to answer. Try doing it now.

WHAT ARE YOU TRYING TO ACHIEVE, NOW, AT THIS MOMENT?

INTENTION IS NOT UNATTAINABLE FUTURE VISION.
INTENTION IS YOUR DIRECTION NOW

A vision is the '*B*' of an '*A to B*' change.

note 6

A vision is aspirational, inspirational, public and articulate. We create a vision to inspire people and to enable alignment. Sometimes it's very detailed. Sometimes it's very simple. Usually it's very distant.

You may be lucky enough to be part of an organisation with a clear vision. If so, what is your particular contribution to it?

'Our vision is for a world free from disease.'

A manager from a medical quality assurance group told me that his intention was for his group of assessors to become consultants and problem-solvers, and not simply critics and inspectors. This intention drove his daily work. It determined how he asked for assessments to be presented. It helped him decide what training he provided to the assessors, and how he spoke about his service to the scientists on the receiving end. This was his positive contribution towards an overall corporate vision of the eradication of disease.

Intention is not a description of a future goal that is perhaps unattainable.

An intention describes a direction you are pursuing now, or a result you expect to see soon, within the next six months, say.

Intention is driving your actions now.

STATING YOUR INTENTION

There may be a company strategy, or a vision. The art of stating your intention is to take these and use them, together with your own career plans and personal values, to find a statement of direction that is meaningful for you and important for your organisation. This isn't always easy.

Getting clear on what you are trying to achieve is a significant part of the work of any change. That doesn't mean it has to take a long time. It just means it's worth doing and takes effort.

here are some questions to help reveal your INTENTION *note 7*

WHAT ARE YOU TRYING TO ACHIEVE HERE (NOW, AT THIS MOMENT)?

WHAT ARE YOU TRYING TO PRESERVE, PROTECT, OR KEEP THE SAME?
WHAT IS IMPORTANT TO YOU ABOUT THAT?

WHAT OR WHO ARE YOU TRYING TO CHANGE?

HOW WILL THE CHANGE BE AN IMPROVEMENT, IN YOUR VIEW?

WHAT'S HAPPENING NOW THAT'S AN EXAMPLE OF WHAT YOU INTEND?

WHAT ASPECTS OF IT ARE IMPORTANT TO YOU?

WHAT'S HAPPENING NOW THAT YOU WANT MORE OF, OR LESS OF?

WHAT DOES 'PROGRESS' MEAN HERE?

WHAT ARE YOUR EXIT CRITERIA: WHAT DO YOU INTEND TO ACCOMPLISH HERE BEFORE YOU CAN LET YOURSELF MOVE ON TO THE NEXT THING?

When you ask these questions you get clearer on what you are trying to achieve, and therefore you can select the right course of action, as the following story illustrates.

CHANGING BUSINESS PROCESSES IN A DISTILLERY

HIM: I want you to facilitate a series of validation workshops. They are to be held in all eight of our European subsidiaries. We have the workshops all set up, dates and places.

ME: *[thinks: European tour! Italy! France!]*
Right! What are we aiming to achieve in these workshops?

HIM: OK, so we've had this huge transformation programme on the go. It's come out with all these proposals for changes. Here's the deck. *[big lever-arch file is produced, containing detailed process diagrams, in colour]* This has all been developed by the project team, reviewed in great detail by audit and legal, and has been approved by the Board.

ME: *[carefully]* It sounds as though the changes have already been agreed.

HIM: *[cheerfully]* Oh yes, the changes have been completely agreed, in great detail as you see, set in stone, so to speak.

ME: So the purpose of the workshops is . . . ?

HIM: We need to get buy-in from the field. We need to run validation workshops to get their buy-in.

ME: *[even more carefully]* Buy-in. Validation. Do they have any choice in the matter, the people in the field? Can they change anything at this stage?

HIM: *[proudly]* No. It's a done deal. It's mandatory.

ME: *[after another careful pause]* So what needs to be done now is communication. We need to tell the field what has been agreed, explain what the new procedures are and why they are important. There is no 'validation' to be done. It's not useful to ask their opinion on decisions which have already been taken. You aren't asking for their view. They can't change anything. What you need is not a series of workshops, but a communication campaign.

HIM: No workshops?

ME: Well, there may be some element of workshop later on, but the important thing now is to communicate what has already been agreed. You need to tell people, clearly and simply, what they have to do. That isn't a validation workshop, that's structured communication, a roadshow, perhaps, combined with training courses, user manuals and audits.

HIM: I see what you mean. Hmm. We haven't got anything to 'workshop'. We don't need a facilitator then?

ME: No, I don't think so.

CLARITY ON INTENTION DRIVES PRECISION IN ACTION

The intention of the manager here was to get the people in the field to comply with a mandatory process. He was not looking for their approval or 'validation'. The time had passed for collecting their ideas in a workshop. When he stated his intention as 'compliance', he saw much more clearly what action he had to take.

INTENTIONS ARE REVEALED BY ACTION

If you think this is all very obvious, then you would be surprised how often, as a consultant, I discover that my clients have embarked on a course of action without being able to state its purpose.

As a result I often help people find the answer to the question 'Why are we doing this?' Sometimes people have a feeling for what they want to do before they quite know why they want to do it. Once we've discovered the intention, we can reinforce the action and make it more precise, as this story shows.

THE MANAGER'S AWAY DAY

MANAGER: I want a Team Away Day *[He's very clear about that. He has already got some dates reserved.]*

ME: Good. What is it you would like to achieve from the Away Day?

MANAGER: I want to get the team together. We are all sales people. We don't get together very often as a team.

ME: I see: a celebration and reunion. Is there anything else? What shifts or changes are you trying to accomplish with this team?

MANAGER: I want them to raise their game. *[He pauses, realising what he has said.]* I want *us* to raise *our* game. We have a huge opportunity here with this client. My sales people, well, some of them, are just chasing opportunities. I want them to be 'Account Managers' in the true sense. I want them to look longer-term than just the next three months. I want them to plan how they are going to develop the business . . .

The manager expanded enthusiastically on this theme. He intended to have a powerful group of people round him. He was keen to develop his team: to encourage them to operate at more senior levels, and to create larger opportunities. In later conversations, he got well beyond the three months and was talking about developing business which would last twenty years.

In this conversation, we'd revealed that he had an intention beyond simply getting the team together to celebrate a successful year. His intention was to have the team 'look longer-term' and to 'raise their game'. This intention directed us to include planning exercises in the meeting, and to collect information on the long-term future of his client. As a result of using this information during planning exercises in the meeting, the team started to change how they saw themselves, and thus adjust their way of operating. If we had not had such a clear intention, we might have had a happy and sociable meeting, but we would not have initiated any changes.

EFFECTIVE ACTION BEGINS WITH THE QUESTION: 'WHAT ARE WE TRYING TO ACHIEVE HERE?'

WHY? ARE WE DOING THIS

REMOVE MISUNDERSTANDING

It might be useful to think:

> *I'm about to do this. When other people see me do it, what intention or motivation are they likely to ascribe to me? Are they right? If not, what is my intention?*

It is sometimes useful to note what your intention is NOT.

Here's an example:

I was in Manchester, in an audio conference with some members of a project team. Their engineering team leader, in a faraway London head office, was on the speaker phone. Her voice came from a domed loudspeaker on the table among the crackling plastic cups. Here is what we heard:

TEAM LEADER: For the next six months, I'm going to be coming up to Manchester every week to see how your project is getting on.

I looked around the table at my end of the phone. I saw eyes rolled to the ceiling, grimaces of irritation and furrowed brows of incomprehension. There were mutterings.

ENGINEER A: *[thinks]* She doesn't trust us.

ENGINEER B: *[thinks]* She thinks we're late.

ENGINEER C: *[thinks]* She's in trouble with the auditors.

ENGINEER D: *[thinks]* We give detailed data to the Programme Office every week. Obviously the Programme Office aren't giving it to her! Or she doesn't trust them? Or she thinks we are lying.

ENGINEER E: *[out loud]* What's all that about then?

The team leader's intention was to make these special engineers feel valued. She wanted to show she cared, by giving them more management attention and time, and visiting them in person.

It would have helped if she had declared her intention. She could have said she wanted to encourage the team and asked them what they needed.

If you don't *declare* your intention, people will *guess* your intention, as the team members did here. The most influential guesses are going to be the ones that feel threatening or critical.

A
SHE DOESN'T TRUST US
B
SHE THINKS WE'RE LYING
SHE'S IN TROUBLE WITH THE AUDITORS
C
SHE THINKS WE'RE LATE
D

"What's all that about then?"
A
B
C
D
E
JANE

DECLARE YOUR INTENTION

When you tell other people what you are trying to achieve:

- you hear yourself say it, which is a useful test for whether you mean it or not;
- you make a commitment;
- you communicate: the other person may be able to help you;
- you stop people having to do the hard work of second-guessing your intentions;
- you open the possibility of learning: the other person may be able to help you see how your intention is or isn't consistent with your values, or your other intentions. They may show you how it fits in with other people's intentions, or how it is different.

So try telling at least one other person what you are trying to achieve.

'I know what I think when I hear what I say'

IS YOUR *'TO DO'* LIST TAKING YOU WHERE YOU WANT IT TO GO? CHECK THAT IT IS

Take some things you are doing now. These might be things that you have in progress or meetings and events you have planned. Look at your diary or To Do list. Use them to reveal your intentions. Check your own self-consistency.

For each item, ask:

- What is it I intend to achieve by doing that?
- Does every To Do item match an intention?

Have you declared your intentions – do other people know why you are doing this?

Would it help if you did tell them?

WHY? ARE WE DOING THIS

?

- *x*
- *why*
- *z*

3 DESCRIBE THE CHANGE

What difference will it make?

Once we have a clear intention, we must discover what needs to change, and what needs to stay the same. We must then state this in a way that drives action.

The messages in this chapter are:

1. A change makes things different:

- state the change you want in terms of 'From' and 'To'
- ensure the 'To' is a specific and clear objective
- make sure that differences are noticeable: state what you want the difference to be

2. Establish continuity during change:
make sure you know what's NOT going to change.

A CHANGE MAKES THINGS DIFFERENT: THERE MUST BE A *FROM* AND A *TO*

If we want to make change happen, then we must know what is meant by 'a change'.

Change makes things different. Look around to see how things are now. After the change, they will be different. There must be a 'From' and there must be a 'To'.

- The *from* describes something that you can see happening now.
- The *to* describes the same thing after the change has happened.
- The *from* and the *to* must be noticeably different from each other.

If you want a change you can't keep everything the same. Some people will find this so obvious as not to be worth stating. Others will nod with recognition, remembering 'change programmes' which are tasked with improving customer satisfaction while maintaining, in a perfect state of stasis:

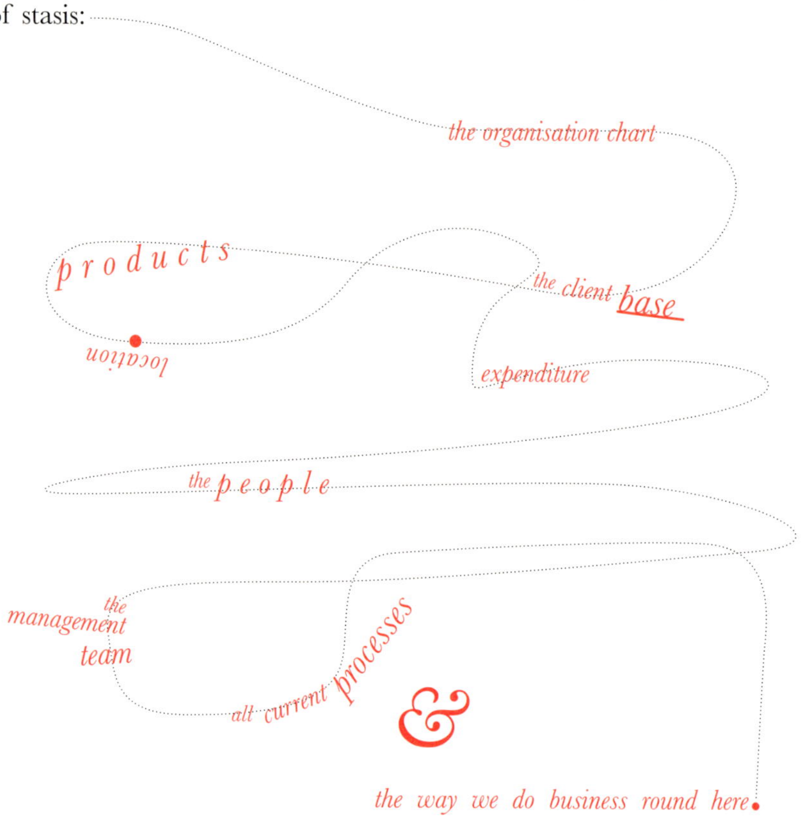

You can't have a change programme which maintains all aspects of the status quo.

If you state the *from* and the *to* you can get co-ordinated action and you can make change happen. If you leave it vague, something might happen, or it might not.

Here is an example from a specialist division of a chemicals manufacturer. They supply bulky liquids and powders, in barrels and containers. A clear expression of *from* and *to* produced action for this division.

A STORY ABOUT PRICING

Sales people complained that it was 'impossible to get a price out of the marketing department'. Customers often called the service centre trying to understand their invoices. Some of the larger customers noticed that different sales people offered different deals, and used this fact to drive down prices. Sales people were rewarded on revenue, and they'd been doing fine. However, the management team of the division were rewarded on profit, and profit had been a bit low recently.

To address all this, and mainly with the intention of driving up profit, the management team called together some sales people, marketing people and service centre staff. This task force gathered data and proposed changes. They wanted to introduce some standardisation into the pricing process, and they wanted the sales people to sell the more profitable products and services.

The task force expressed the change in terms of *from* and *to*. They then communicated this to people affected by the change.

from [*today*]	*to* [*future*]
Over 50% of the purchase orders processed by our service centre contain prices that are not on the published price list.	100% of purchase orders correspond to the published price list. No special cases, no special deals, no exceptions.
Sales people sell as many products as possible to reach their revenue targets.	Sales people balance revenue and profit.

Of course that provoked an explosion of questions, such as: 'How are we going to do that?' But the task force held firm and obtained agreement about the change they wanted to achieve. Meanwhile they, and others, were already finding solutions, and articulating other changes that made this possible:

from [*today*]	*to* [*future*]
The price list covers only our products. Services, such as delivery to quayside, or special customer labelling, are priced by the sales person as part of the sales negotiation.	Every product and every service has a standard price on the price list.
Sales people have to phone the pricing centre to get the prices.	The price list is on the sales people's laptops, updated daily by downloads.
Sales people don't know the product profitability.	Profit information is available to salespeople.

The last item was highly contentious. It was not implemented. Some groups felt that product profitability was a commercial secret, not to be published outside the finance department.

The other major difficulty was that sales people were using the ambiguities in the pricing process to strike special deals with customers. They resented the removal of this flexibility: 'If the prices are standard, then how do I negotiate?' This was resolved by initially offering some small flexibility in the price list.

As time passed, sales people learned how to sell at standard prices.

THE CLEAR EXPRESSION OF *from* AND *to* PRODUCES ACTION

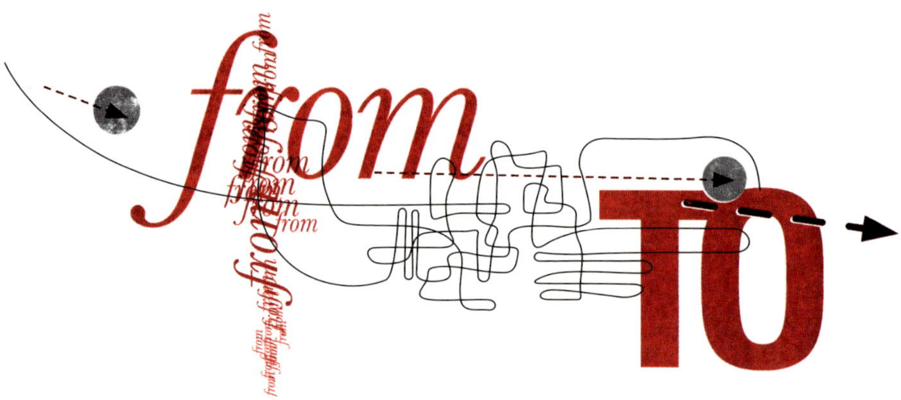

In this story, the clear statement of the *from* and *to* provoked an outcry, but it also produced action. Things DID change. The management team regained control of customer end prices, and so could manage for profit.

The task force would have got nowhere if it had rested with a general statement: *'Our mission is to improve the pricing process.'*

They would have provoked no outcry, but also made no progress, if they had obscured their intention with management-speak: *'Our customer-centric change programme will drive profitability by streamlining the interaction between the customers and the business.'*

Such cautious pronouncements might be necessary to get an initiative started, but they don't make change happen.

WHEN ARTICULATING *FROM* AND *TO*, KEEP IT SMALL AND SPECIFIC

When describing your change, it helps to keep it limited in scope.

If you don't feel bold enough to specify what is going to happen to the whole division, then state what's going to happen in, say, the Warrington Distribution Centre. You can restrict your scope to purchases under £250, or to desktops that are directly connected to your server. You could state the *from* and *to* for just one of your product lines, or just one type of customer.

Be clear about a small part of the change, rather than vague about a wide scope. Even if you only succeed in making a change in one specific area, at least you will have achieved something. You can publicise your success and others will follow.

Many change initiatives flounder because they are too big. People are more likely to understand what you are talking about if you keep it limited. If you talk about the whole company, people feel it's all rather conceptual and few will engage. If you mention the Warrington Distribution Centre, your concepts become real. You'll certainly engage the people in Warrington, and others will know you mean business.

THE PEOPLE DOING THE WORK KNOW WHAT HAS TO CHANGE

Whatever it is you are trying to achieve, whether it's cost saving, improved service or an efficient office move, the people whose daily lives are affected are the people who know what has to change. Talk to them, spend time with them, use their experience and practical knowledge to work out what has to change. With them, discover what has to be different when your intention becomes a reality. Ask: what is the *from* and what is the *to*?

questions which help identify the FROM and TO

WHAT NEEDS TO BE DIFFERENT AROUND HERE WHEN MY INTENTION IS REALISED?

from .... [*today*]	*to* .... [*future*]

WHAT WILL PEOPLE BE DOING THAT THEY ARE NOT DOING NOW?

from .... [*today*]	*to* .... [*future*]

WHAT WILL PEOPLE NOT BE DOING THAT THEY ARE DOING NOW?

from [*today*] | *to* [*future*]

WHAT WILL THEY BE SAYING IN THE FUTURE AND HOW IS THAT DIFFERENT FROM WHAT THEY ARE SAYING NOW?

WHERE WILL THEY BE GOING? HOW WILL THEIR DIARIES BE DIFFERENT?

WHAT WILL HAVE STOPPED?

from [*today*] | *to* [*future*]

IF I TOOK A VIDEO NOW AND A VIDEO AFTER MY INTENTION HAS BECOME REALITY, WHAT DIFFERENCE WOULD I SEE OR HEAR?

from [*today*] *to* [*future*]

WHAT WILL THERE BE MORE OF OR LESS OF?
HOW MUCH MORE OR LESS?

WHAT WILL THIS CHANGE CREATE THAT ISN'T THERE ALREADY?
HOW WILL I KNOW THAT IT'S THERE?

WHAT WILL THIS CHANGE REMOVE THAT'S THERE NOW?
HOW WILL I KNOW THAT IT HAS GONE?

from [*today*] *to* [*future*]

from .... *[today]* **?** *to* .... *[future]*

from .... *[today]* *to* .... *[future]*

THE *TO* MUST BE **SMART**

The principles above are those used to define 'SMART objectives'. A change programme must have a *from* and a *to*, and the *to* must be in the form of a SMART objective. SMART is an acronym. It stands for:

note 8

Specific:	*This change* in *this part* of the business
Measurable:	Visible impact, noticeable effect
Achievable:	I can envisage it happening, it's not impossible
Results-based:	It describes an outcome, not a process
Timely:	I can specify an end-date

Setting out SMART objectives for your particular endeavour makes co-ordinated action possible.

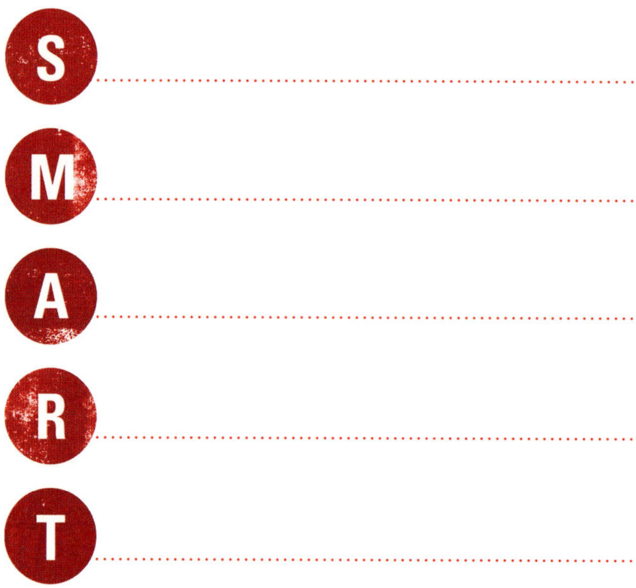

NICK WALROND IMPROVES ACCOUNT MANAGEMENT

Nick Walrond wanted to improve account management as part of his overall growth strategy for Sanderson, the recruitment company of which he is managing director. He was effective in doing this because he had a precise idea of what 'improved account management' looked like. He gained this precision from spending time with account managers as they did their work. *note 9*

In his new model, account managers would:

- Use their customers' recruitment systems: use the customers' templates, and operate the customers' approval process.
- Maintain relationships with all the people in their customers' business who are involved in recruitment: procurement, human resources, the hiring manager, the candidates' supervisors and the senior managers.
- Systematically maintain contact with candidates, once placed, to obtain further information about the customers.

Each of these is 'Specific' to the account manager's customer. Each is 'Measurable', because you can see and test if someone is doing it or not. They are all 'Achievable' since the account managers are in control of the people involved. They are all 'Results-based' because they describe what things will look like after the change has been accomplished.

Nick set out timeframes for when he expected this to be in place, and formats for the information he expected the account managers to maintain. As a result of this precision, they could work out what to do. Nick's SMART objectives drove co-ordinated action.

SMART OBJECTIVES DRIVE ACTION

here are some **SMART** objectives

eg

'By 31 July this year, all purchase orders processed by our Cheltenham invoicing centre will contain only price-list prices. There will be no special prices, and no discounts.'

'This new business service will be up and running in Swindon at the end of this year, with at least one customer contract in place.'

'By 1 June there will be a fully staffed assessment centre in place and we will have used it to select 30 graduates for September start.'

'By 7 April there will be in place a permanent management team. This means: all posts filled, no gaps in the team, no interims, no consultants, nobody wanting to move on to other jobs.'

'In the next six months, starting now, we will have at least one period of continuous service availability that lasts longer than three months.'

OBJECTIVES MUST BE

S P E C I F I C

& MEASURABLE

The table below shows some examples of objectives that are not SMART, and gives ideas on how to make them SMART:

this objective is not **SMART**	it is not **SMART** because...	here's how it might be **SMART**ened up
We will standardise our purchasing procedures	It's an activity not an outcome. It's not measurable. I can't test I've done it. It's not specific. We have many purchasing procedures.	By the beginning of next financial year, all purchases over £250: • will be made by company invoice only; • will specify a cost code; and • will be approved by the budget holder.
We will raise awareness of our company strategy	It's not measurable. *Awareness* is invisible: I cannot know when it's 'raised'. It's not specific. We have strategies at company level, BU level, store level. *Raise awareness* is a process, not an outcome.	After this communication campaign, all front-line staff in our retail outlets will be able to answer correctly the following three questions: • Who are our target customers? • How will our company change over the next year? • What are we doing as a company to combat global warming?
We will roll out the corporate portal worldwide	It's not measurable. How will I tell if it's rolled out? It's not achievable. We have 121 subsidiaries, and many colleagues have no web access.	By 31 December, we will have the corporate portal in use in at least 10 subsidiaries. 'In use' means at least 20% of the workforce is accessing it every day.

The statements in the left-hand column on the opposite page are good starting points. They represent intentions. To drive action, they need to be SMART.

A common reason why change doesn't happen is because people tell you that the change you want is 'already in place'. 'Nobody need do anything!' Purchasing procedures are already 'standard' – it's just that there are currently rather a lot of standards. People are already aware of the company strategy – it's just that we've all got a different idea of what the strategy is.

The power of the SMART objective is that it forces you to think through what 'test' might show that your change is accomplished. You can then easily ascertain whether the change you want is indeed 'already in place'.

The SMART objective is the *to*. If you want to make a difference then you need also to specify the *from* side. Make sure that the *from* and the *to* are different.

WHAT'S GOING TO STAY THE SAME?

It's always worth thinking about, and stating, what's going to stay the same throughout the proposed change. Sometimes the purpose of the proposed change is to preserve some important aspect of the status quo.

THE 'ULRICH KAUFMANN' STORY

The business unit manager listened to my presentation in silence, arms folded. Afterwards, I went up to see him in his office on the 14th floor. 'Ulrich Kaufmann' is German, a strong man, silhouetted against his office window. His office block towers over the chemical plant that produces the reactive compound he sells. You can smell the clean chemicals in the air.

'Jane,' he says calmly. I can't see his expression because he is outlined against the window. 'You are a consultant,' he tells me. 'Your work is change. I am a businessman. My business unit delivered a certain profit this year. It did so last year, and the same the year before. The company counts on us also for identical profits next year. They have placed my business unit in the category "Core", which means we deliver a solid profit and which also gives us certain other advantages. I do not want a change. I want to "preserve the status quo", as you put it. We must continue to return the same profit every year. We must do so even though the patents on our most profitable molecules will expire in five years' time. It is possible that you can propose some measures which will protect our position. In this case you can count on my support. But I do not want a change to the status quo. Do you understand?'

I understood, and I remembered. I still remember. His penetrating words taught me the importance of stating what is staying the same. 'I do not want a change to the status quo.'

IT IS IMPORTANT TO STATE WHAT WILL STAY THE SAME

here are some questions to help you work out
WHAT'S STAYING THE SAME?

WHAT DO YOU WANT TO PRESERVE OR PROTECT?

WHAT MUST NOT BE LOST DURING THIS TRANSITION?

WHAT IS UNTOUCHED BY THIS CHANGE?

examples of **ANSWERS** to these questions

eg

Our profitability will stay the same.

We will uphold our customer service standards.

We will retain our market share.

Our team of in-house specialists will remain.

We will maintain our existing discount schemes with our three major customers.

We will preserve our 'A' rating with the regulator.

You will be able to take all of your annual leave.

This year's sales commissions are not affected by this change.

We will still be working on the Thames Valley site, possibly in a different building.

The customer facing brands will remain the same: Toot Sweets stay in the same packaging.

No jobs will be lost as a result of this change.

The statements about what's staying the same may seem obvious. But this is an instance where it's a good idea to state the obvious.

Here's why we state what's not going to change:

- Setting boundaries helps people be more creative.
- It's important to keep what's good.
- By showing that there will be continuity you reduce anxiety.

These are explored in more detail below.

SETTING BOUNDARIES HELPS PEOPLE BE CREATIVE

If you don't set constraints people generally assume that the field of play is smaller than it actually is, and so their creativity is stifled. By saying what's out of bounds you concentrate people's minds on what's in scope. People can then propose ambitious schemes within the constraints you have set.

SAVING TIME IN A BANK BRANCH

A group of us had been tasked with speeding up processes in the branches of a high street bank. The area manager had been explicit about the constraints: 'No changes to the credit check rules, and no changes to units outside the branch.' He drew a heavy black circle on a flipchart to represent that boundary. He pointed to the blank space inside the circle. 'Everything else INSIDE the branch is in scope.'

The staff from one of the branches had a great idea for how to speed up mortgage applications. These currently needed a three-part application form requiring three customer signatures. Using scissors and glue, the branch staff gleefully redesigned the form. They invented a two-part form requiring only two signatures.

'But,' said one participant dolefully, 'audit will never agree.' We were on the point of dropping the idea when somebody pointed out that this proposal didn't change the credit check rules, and was entirely INSIDE the branch. It was therefore in scope. She suggested we contact audit and ask them about the proposal.

To everyone's surprise, 'audit' arrived in person: an eager man with spectacles. He was delighted to be involved 'so early in the process'. He was enthusiastic about their idea of simplifying the application form. The simplification actually made his job easier, he said, and 'How about we look at getting it down to just one sheet of paper and one signature?' He grabbed the scissors and the glue.

BEING EXPLICIT ABOUT BOUNDARIES ENCOURAGES BOLD INNOVATION

People constrain themselves to a small space, just to be 'on the safe side' and not go over any edges. So, to help them know where the 'edge' is: say what's NOT going to change.

DURING ANY CHANGE IT'S IMPORTANT TO KEEP WHAT'S GOOD

We don't want to lose or damage processes that are already working. We might want to build on things that are already happening. Many people may already be making progress in the direction we want. We must say what's going to stay the same, so we remember to keep it, or build on it. *note 10*

During any change, some people will not be part of the razzmatazz of the change programme. They will just be carrying on as normal, preserving continuity and maintaining service. We must acknowledge and value their contribution, just as we value the contribution from those people who have to accomplish change.

SANDERSON'S DELIVERY TEAM STAYS THE SAME

Earlier in this chapter, I described Nick Walrond's SMART objectives for changing the activities of his account management team. This was part of his overall programme to grow Sanderson's business.

Sanderson has an account management team, who find vacancies, and a delivery team, who find candidates.

Delivery was working well: they already maintained long-term relationships with candidates and had a good knowledge of their marketplace. They provided stability during the change. It was important that changes in the account management processes did not disrupt the good work of the delivery team.

Through his management team, and by direct conversations in the office, Nick kept the delivery team up to date with his intentions. He told them that their good work was valued, their team structure would stay the same, and that their people would benefit from the increased business that would flow from the enhanced sales capability of their colleagues in account management. Obviously, the delivery team would experience some changes, such as new processes relating to account management, but mostly their work would remain the same.

By making it clear what was staying the same, Nick was able to focus his management attention on achieving successful change in one area of his company, while retaining the support of other areas.

IT'S IMPORTANT TO KEEP WHAT IS GOOD

REDUCE ANXIETY BY SHOWING THAT THERE WILL BE CONTINUITY

Continuity is calming. Change is exciting. Create a balance by placing effort into both continuity and change. Make sure that your presentations, conversations and measurement systems mention those aspects which are not changing. People can then see some continuity between the past and the future, which is helpful during uncertain times.

Despite this world of 'ever-increasing change', some things stay the same. The Number 8 tram still leaves Barfüsserplatz. The bells of St Clement's *note 11* still chime 'Oranges and Lemons'. And Ulrich Kaufmann's business unit is still turning in its steady profit.

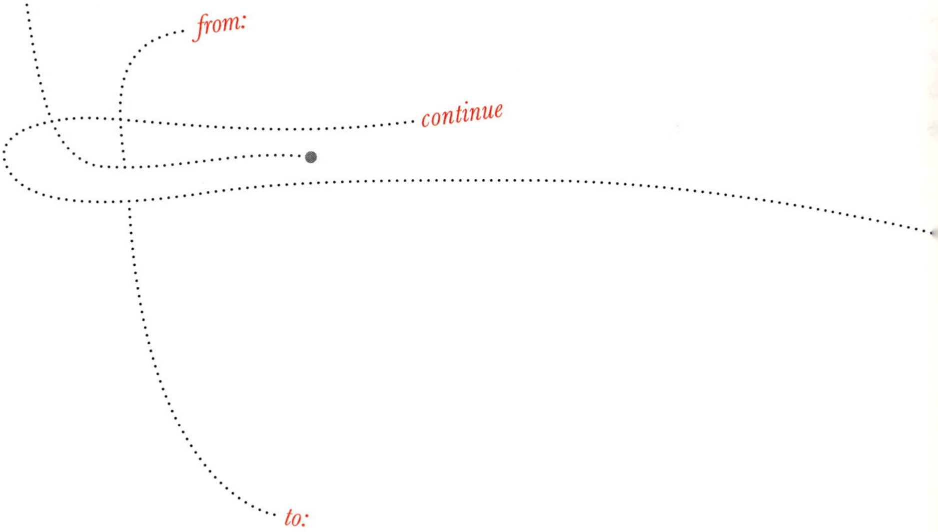

8

8

8

4 CHOOSE EFFECTIVE ACTION

What shall I do?

From the previous chapters we're clear what it is we are trying to achieve, we've stated what needs to change and what needs to stay the same. Now we have to decide what to do (this chapter), then we've got to do it (next chapter). *note 12*

The messages in this chapter are:

1. Choose action not activity:

- do the things which make a difference, not the things which make no difference

2. Choose the most effective action:

- do the things which have the biggest effect and the greatest chance of success

3. Choose the most direct action:

- do the things which most directly deliver the outcome you want

CHARACTERISTICS OF ACTION

Since action is needed to make change happen, it's important that we are able clearly to distinguish action from those activities which might look like action.

Here are some ways to recognise action:

Action is finite

It has a beginning, middle and end.

Action is self-eliminating

Once you've done it, it's done, and doesn't have to be done again.

Action has an effect, and not doing it has an effect also

If you do the action, something will happen. If you don't do it, something different will happen.

Action is usually irreversible for all practical purposes

An action usually takes about as much effort to undo as to do. If it's easily reversed, then nothing much has happened, and no action has occurred.

For example, recruiting John into the post of programme manager is an action. But until John has arrived, started work and met the staff and customers, the whole process is reversible. While we are writing the job description, interviewing candidates, and making the offer, we can change our mind at any stage and with little effort. Even once he's accepted, he can change his mind. However, once he's arrived, met his direct reports and engaged with customers, then it is a lot of effort to throw the process into reverse. Therefore we are keen to get to this 'irreversible' action point as fast as possible, so that change happens.

Action takes effort: it won't 'just happen anyway'

If it 'just happens anyway' it's not an action, it's an inevitability. *You are not making change happen; you are simply watching change happen.* This is a rewarding activity, but it is not what this book is about.

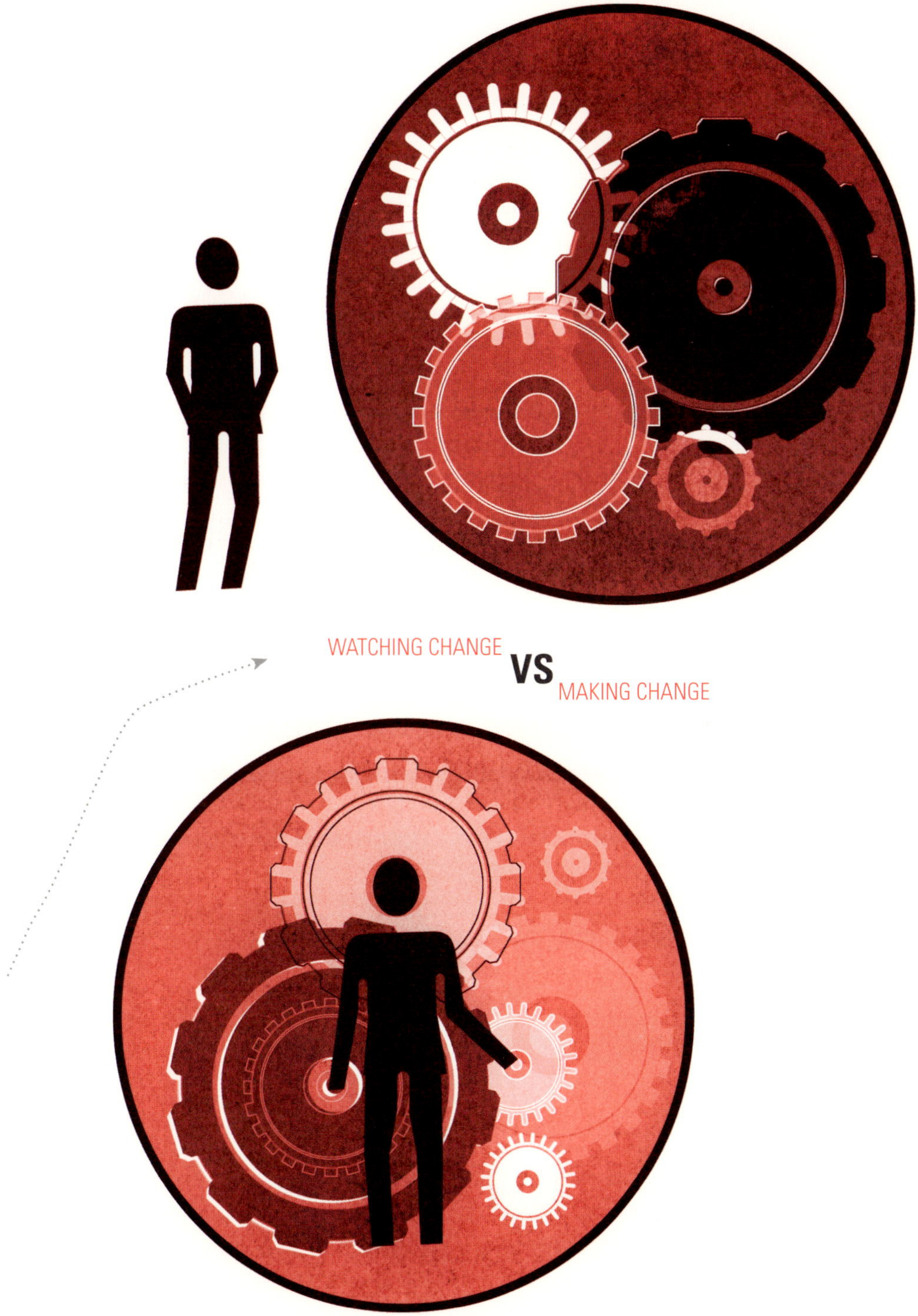
WATCHING CHANGE
VS
MAKING CHANGE

Action closes down options

Doing this means not doing that. If you want to check that a proposal to do something is genuinely an action, ask: 'If we choose to do that, what are we choosing *not* to do?'

If it's a genuine action there will be a real answer to that question.

Action also means that you have to stop dreaming of all the different possibilities and start working on just one of them. This takes an effort of will.

When we recruit John into the programme manager position, we have to stop dreaming about the possibility that one of the existing team will take the job, or that we can save the budget and manage without a programme manager. These options are removed when John takes up the post.

This is progress. If all the possibilities stay open all the time, then nothing is happening.

CHOOSE ACTION NOT ACTIVITY

It's easy to get involved in things that look like action but are not action. In the next three sections we look at three categories of activity: all valuable and important to a successful business, but which are not action and which do not make change happen:

- Preparation for action
- Support for action
- Maintaining the status quo

If you want to make change happen, you must be alert to the distinction between action, which is what makes change happen, and other activities which don't. Avoid getting caught up endlessly in support, preparation and maintenance activities. Take action instead.

'Preparation for action' is not action

Mike works in a big corporation. He wants to turn his research group into a self-sustaining business in explosives testing and explosion containment.

He has:

- studied the market
- created a business plan
- investigated technologies that he could use
- discussed his ideas with potential new staff members

This is all important work, but nothing has happened yet. Mike and his team have been busy, but they haven't yet made a difference.

Studying, planning, investigating, generating ideas, taking advice: all of these are good preparations for action. But they are not action. The action occurs when something changes.

If Mike wants something to happen, he has to take action, for example:

- close a contract with a customer
- secure funding from the corporation
- purchase equipment
- recruit staff

These actions are different in nature from the preparation activities which preceded them.

'Support for action' is not action

For any action there are many supporting activities. These activities are necessary to the action. Our job, as change agents, is to make sure that those supporting activities do not become ends in themselves. The question always is: Can the action happen now?

The question is not:

'Have we done a good market survey?'

but

'Have we done enough of a market survey to make a purchase now?'

Here follow some examples of such supporting activities. There are plenty more.

ACTION	SUPPORTING ACTIVITIES (examples)
Appointing someone to a post	• Writing a job description • Listing evaluation criteria • Conducting interviews
Buying or selling something, trading, money changing hands, goods changing ownership	• Surveying the market • Making a list of goods • Writing a cost/benefit case
Creating, making or building an object (a computer system, a machine tool, a bus shelter, a production line, a system of filing trays . . .)	• Specifying requirements • Designing • Planning • Assessing risk • Visioning
Disciplining someone for non-compliance with standards	• Writing standards • Publishing guidelines • Monitoring compliance • Gathering and analysing data
Removing something: mergers, elimination of a brand, disbanding a project team, terminating a contract	• Discussing scenarios • Brainstorming options • Setting out implications • Taking a decision
Requesting: asking someone to do something and obtaining a commitment or a refusal	• Holding exploratory conversations • Describing a problem • Complaining about a process • Admiring a role model
Mending, curing, repairing something: the email system, the invoicing process	• Process mapping • Analysing costs

ACTIONS:

actions

ACTIONS:

actions

adapt

adopt

add

deliver

demolish

dismiss

REMOVE

REPAIR

REPLACE

Support and preparation activities are essential to achieving successful change. However they are support for action, not substitutes for it. We have to keep them clearly directed at producing action. If we can go straight to the action, then let's do that.

Is that process map really necessary?

'Activities to maintain the status quo' are not action

In addition to all the activities which support action, there are many activities which are needed to keep the existing systems working. They are important to any successful business, but they do not cause change. You'll need to recognise and appreciate these maintenance activities. You will want to use them after you've made your change, to make your change stick and to monitor its effect.

Here is a list of some activities which maintain the status quo:

- maintaining equipment
- reporting service levels
- checking security passes
- keeping the database up-to-date
- renewing existing contracts
- classifying, filing and organising information
- monitoring expenditure

Any of these can be an important precursor to action. But whereas such activities are a spur to action, they are not action. They don't, of themselves, change anything. Monitoring expenditure does not cause a reduction in costs unless someone does something with the monitoring data. Reporting service levels does not deliver better customer service unless someone takes action as a result of the reports they receive. Collecting data and maintaining systems are significant and useful activities: but for change to happen, we need action.

CHOOSE THE MOST EFFECTIVE ACTION

Of all the actions you could take to make your change happen, make sure you put your main effort into the things that are going to have a big effect and are going to work. The best course of action may be obvious. If not, you could try classifying your options:

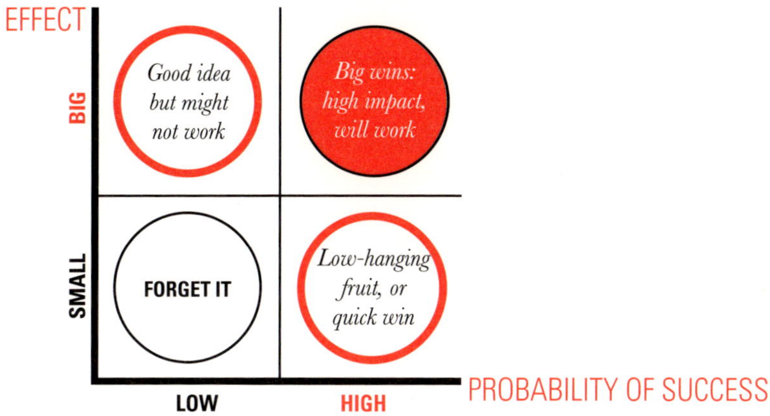

- Do the things which are going to make the most progress towards turning your intention into reality.
- Do them now.
- Balance your portfolio of action and manage your risk by also choosing some easy actions which have a small effect. But don't shirk the big ones.

ROLF FISCHER'S HOTEL

Rolf Fischer is the proprietor of the Hôtel Jean-Jacques Rousseau in Geneva. When he took over the hotel he had a clear intention to grow the business. An early objective was to increase the room occupancy throughout the whole week. He already had a number of valued guests who came as delegates to the World Health Organization and other international organisations based in Geneva. Meeting delegates tend to stay during the week and leave on Friday. The hotel was relatively empty at weekends. Rolf took a balanced portfolio of actions to increase occupancy. *note 13*

Here are some of the immediate, low-risk actions he took which had a small but worthwhile effect:

- He initiated a dialogue with the Geneva tourist office so that they would send weekend visitors to the hotel.
- He encouraged the staff to help the guests during their stay. Staff provide Swiss power adapters for guests' mobile phones, and give advice on local restaurants, for example. Guests who are not confident in the local languages can therefore feel at home and will come back.
- He designed a simple invoice, with all rates and taxes included, so that customers have no surprises when they leave, and are therefore more likely to return.

The most courageous action, and the one which was going to have the biggest effect, was the decision to renovate the hotel. Rolf put his main effort, and much of his own time, into this expensive and long-term endeavour. He embarked on this decisively, starting by redecorating the reception area to give a fresh and bright atmosphere on arrival. This immediately received appreciative comments from guests, who then sympathetically tolerated the plasterers on the stairways and the plumbers in the hall.

Rolf talks to guests to get their reaction and he carefully monitors occupancy rates. His business is now succeeding. Occupancy rates are much higher – very often 100% – and profitability has increased.

DO THE THINGS WHICH HAVE THE BIGGEST EFFECT AND THE GREATEST CHANCE OF SUCCESS

CHOOSE THE MOST DIRECT ACTION

note 14 Do the things which most directly deliver the outcome you want.

When you have a change to accomplish, think: Is there a way we can do this, or a piece of this, immediately?

Can we just go and tell people what we are proposing and try it?

NIGEL PHILLIPPS, MANAGING DIRECTOR OF UNITY

NIGEL PHILLIPPS TAKES DIRECT ACTION

Nigel Phillipps is the managing director of Unity, a software engineering company. His offices are in the restored Bristol docklands. With his management team he had resolved that they needed to find more customers. *note 15*

Nigel and his team are engineers. Engineers like to analyse. They spent a lot of time working out where the customers might be. They did a geographical breakdown of customer distribution, an analysis by product area, by industry and by size.

Engineers are good at building things, so Nigel and his engineers started designing new products. They made prototypes. They formed an alliance with a company in a complementary field.

All of these were efforts aimed in the general direction of marketing. They were useful activities, but indirect.

Nigel is a surfer. He confidently launches himself into the waves of the North Cornish coast. At work, he is comfortable in his office, surrounded by his team, in a laid-back environment.

It took courage for him to get on the phone, put on a suit, and launch himself into sales. He met potential customers and asked for business. When Nigel took this direct action, he found the customers he wanted.

TAKE DIRECT ACTION

'Lean Manufacturing' is a systematic approach to eliminate unnecessary work from manufacturing processes. The idea is to: *note 16*

- discover what the customer values and will pay for; and then
- direct all activities strictly towards adding value for the customer, removing those that are unnecessary.

Similarly, we can practise Lean Thinking in change management. As we have seen, we must:

- declare our intention; and then
- align our actions strictly with that intention, removing any activity that is not necessary to make our change happen.

This direct action is the principle behind the 'Action Lab': a tool used to make change happen. The idea here is to create a microcosm of the changed business in a localised physical space, such as a large room. So, for example, when a team of us were trying to change the method of oil distribution in a region, we assembled a team of experienced people from each of the functions involved. Our team members took real oil orders from customers and operated the essential elements of the proposed new process. Each day we improved the process after a review of 'lessons learned' the previous evening. The team members used the facility to demonstrate the process to other people in their functions, who offered further suggestions and improvements. Our room became a training facility whereby new processes were demonstrated and adopted across the company.

CHOOSE EFFECTIVE ACTION – PRACTICAL APPLICATION

So now you can compare your proposed course of action with your intention:

- CHOOSE ACTION NOT ACTIVITY

  Will this action get your change to happen?

  - or are you getting stuck in preparatory work, support work, or maintaining the existing system?

- CHOOSE EFFECTIVE ACTION

  Are you doing the most effective thing?

  - or are you burning too much energy and time on a series of small endeavours?

- CHOOSE DIRECT ACTION

  Have you identified the simplest, smallest number of steps to make it happen?

  - or are there intermediate steps you could eliminate?

ACTION
ACTIVITY

5 GET INTO ACTION

A gift of great
utility
is common copability:
The knack of getting
each thing done
before the grind
has spoiled the fun.

• *'The Gift' from* Grooks *by Piet Hein* *note 17*

This chapter is about doing it. It is about making the important transition from *'thinking about it'* to *'doing it'*.

So the simple message of this chapter is 'Do it':

- teach yourself to move to action
- don't delay, don't procrastinate
- don't get caught up in planning, analysing, preparing

'A good decision executed quickly beats
a brilliant decision implemented slowly'

• *Paul Rogers and Marcia Blenko* *note 18*

DO IT.

DO IT: HOW TO GET YOURSELF TO DO THINGS

If you have a clear intention, an objective you want, and a course of action which leads there, then moving to action should be straightforward and require no effort.

However, sometimes this isn't straightforward and does require effort. Distractions crowd in. Secondary objectives suddenly become appealing. Shall I place that online grocery order? Read my email? Clear out my desk drawer? Investigate what those people are looking at over there? Should I do risk assessment first? Clear it with my boss? With my peers? All of these seem suddenly more attractive than taking the action you had decided upon: picking up the phone and making an appointment with a customer to offer them your new product.

It's worth paying attention to how you get yourself into action. Sometimes it's easy to take action and sometimes it's difficult, so notice what makes action easy for you, and use that awareness to help ease the difficult times.

Here are some ways people get into action. Different things work for different people and in different circumstances. What works for you?

USE YOUR MIND

Remember why you are doing this: restate your intention

Write your intention at the top of your To Do list. Remind yourself of how this action will further your intention. Tell yourself and others. Remember that this action is taking you in a direction you want to go, to create a change you want.

Stop using energy thinking about it;
redirect the energy into doing it

Do it. Just walk into the open-plan office and talk to him. Just pick up the phone and dial. I find it helps to write down the first dozen words I am going to say.

Think 'It's my job'

It may be easier to take action 'in role' than it is to take action as 'me'.

'Social gatherings aren't my thing,' a managing director told me, 'but I realised it's part of my job. I have to act the part, so I put on my dinner jacket, and went to the evening event. I met new customers – it was surprisingly easy.'

Remember that actions are finite

Anticipate the end. Once you've done it, it's done, and it won't have to be done again. So get on with it.

note 19 *' It's about treating change like removing a Band-aid. No hesitation. No delay. One quick movement. Rip. Sting. Done. '*

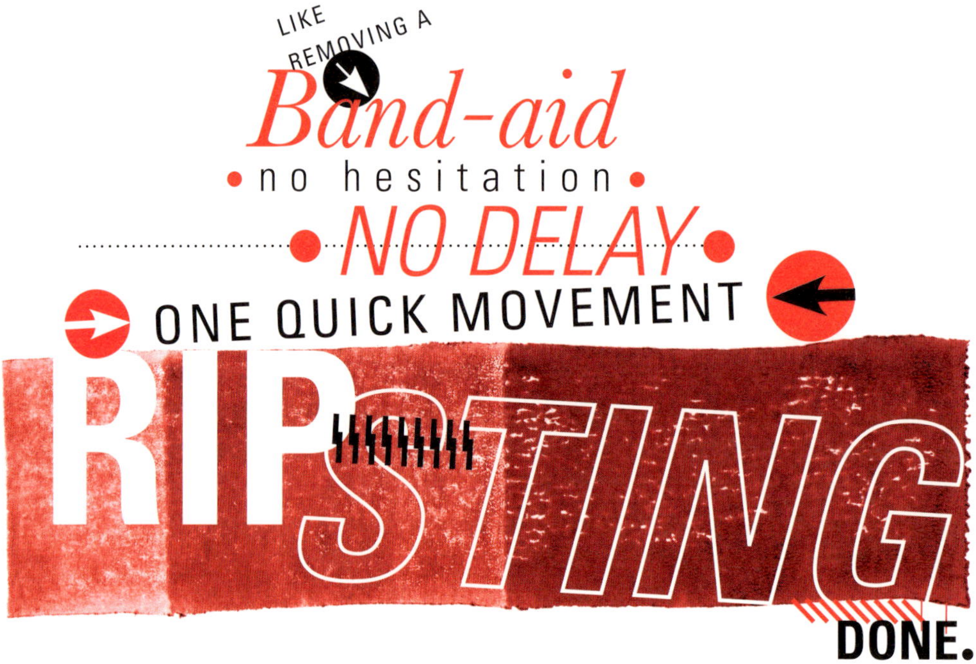

USE OTHER PEOPLE

Ask someone to manage you

Tell a peer, a friend or your boss that it will be done by 3 pm. Ask them to come for a demonstration. If they are a real friend, they'll drop by a while before the deadline to check that you have started.

Do it for someone

Some of us find it easier to do something for someone else than to do it simply for ourselves. Like non-athletes who run marathons to benefit a charity, hold in mind the people who will benefit from your action. Do it for them.

Tell a large number of people you will do it

If you've made a commitment to a lot of people then the shame of saying you didn't try will outweigh the effort of doing it. If a senior manager goes on a roadshow and tells 300 employees that she is going to invest in site improvements, then she had better get on and do it, or she's going to have to face 300 disappointed people next time around.

Get help

Just tell someone what you intend to do, and ask for help.

FIND AN ATTRACTOR

Find something in the action to enjoy, give yourself a treat to pull you in

Arrange for something pleasant and easy to enjoy alongside the effort and difficulty of taking action. Have the difficult meeting in a pleasant place, or post the risky request from a letter box next to a favourite coffee shop. Wear favourite clothes or special socks – like athletes do.

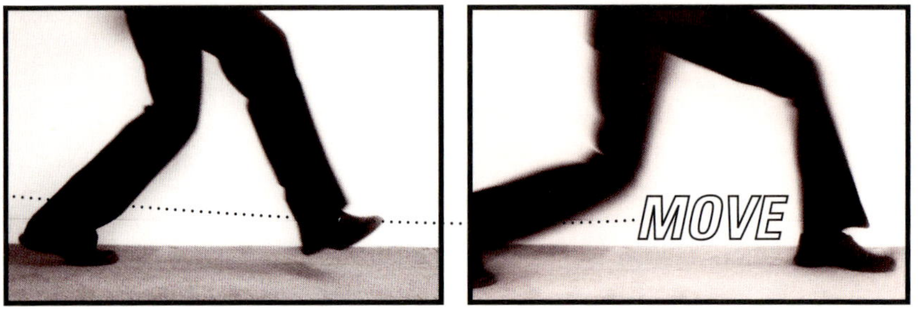

GIVE YOURSELF NO CHOICE

Do nothing else: concentrate only on the main action which makes progress with your objective

If you need to make a difficult phone call, allow yourself to do nothing else until you have made that call.

If you need to create something, stand there, with the materials, until you start picking them up and doing something with them.

Trap yourself

Tell your counter-party you have an important matter to discuss. Tell them what it is. Set a time – or go over there right now. Now you can't get out of it.

Here is Raymond Chandler, creator of Philip Marlowe and author of novels and screenplays, writing about how he gets himself to do things.

> *The important thing is that there should be a space of time, say four hours a day at least, when a professional writer doesn't do anything else but write. He doesn't have to write, and if he doesn't feel like it he shouldn't try. He can look out of the window or stand on his head or writhe on the floor, but he is not to do any other positive thing, not read, not write letters, glance at magazines, or write checks. Either write or nothing. It's the same principle as keeping order in a school. If you make the pupils behave, they will learn something just to keep from being bored. I find it works. Two very simple rules. A. You don't have to write. B. You can't do anything else. The rest comes of itself.*

note 20

Here's an example of a businessman just getting out there and doing it.

NICK WALROND GETS INTO ACTION: SELLING A NEW PRODUCT TO CUSTOMERS

To further his intention to grow the business at Sanderson, Nick decided that his recruitment company should set up a new venture. The existing agency business provided people by the day or hour. This new business would sell self-contained assignments to customers. In the new business the value proposition was that Nick would take on some of the risk inherent in people-intensive activities: 'You want Windows XP rolled out in six weeks? We will roll out XP – we'll decide how many people it will take and what skill levels. You pay us a fixed price for the job.'

In the traditional model, his customer would decide they wanted five desktop engineers, two business analysts and a project manager, and hire each of those people individually by the day. Sanderson traditionally offered the client a selection of candidates from their pool, and the customer made their choice. In the new model, Nick's company would take some of the risk, and so could charge a bit more. It was also less hassle for both Nick and the customer.

However, it was a risk and a shift from Sanderson's traditional positioning. 'So how did you do it?' I asked Nick. 'What did you do?'

Nick was rather puzzled by the question. 'I just went and sold it,' he said.

'How did you find the motivation: you had to go and sell to a customer a product you had not sold before, which posed risks to your business? Wasn't that difficult?'

'Not really,' said Nick. 'I am ambitious. I knew I wanted to grow the company and this was a way to do it. It wasn't a completely new product: we had the people. I was just bespoking it with the customer. Finding a new way to package it which worked for them and for us.'

He did find a way of bespoking it. The offer was taken up. He found other customers who wanted to work in this model. This product line became the new brand Intelligent Consulting. *note 21*

DON'T DELAY, DON'T PROCRASTINATE, DON'T OVERDO THE PLANNING

A classic passage which illustrates the difference between 'talking about it' and 'doing it' is this Theodore Roosevelt speech:

> *It is not the critic who counts, not the one who points out how the strong man stumbled or how the doer of deeds might have done them better. The credit belongs to the man who is actually in the arena, whose face is marred with sweat and dust and blood; who strives valiantly; who errs and comes short again and again; who knows the great enthusiasms, the great devotions, and spends himself in a worthy cause; who, if he wins, knows the triumph of high achievement; and who, if he fails, at least fails while daring greatly, so that his place shall never be with those cold and timid souls who know neither victory nor defeat.*

note 22

Taking action is not complicated, but it takes effort. Sometimes, to avoid effort, we make it complicated. People who take action take risk, and so need courage and strength. In business we may not have the 'sweat and dust and blood' that Roosevelt describes, but we still need to dare greatly. It takes courage to step out of the theory and into the arena.

ONE QUICK MOVEMENT

RIP

STING

DONE.

6 BE AWARE

The completest knowledge of the laws of nature does not carry with it the power of prediction nor of mastery over nature. If the universe is a machine, its levers and wheels are too fine for our hands to manipulate. We can learn and guide its large-scale motions only. Beneath our veiled sight it quivers in eternal unrest.

• *Max Born* note 23

Previous chapters have described taking action in the direction of a stated intention. This chapter emphasises the importance of noticing what's going on while you are in action:

- the effect of your action is unpredictable: place your attention on what *is* going on, not on what *should be* going on
- all action is participative: remain in contact with people affected by the change: listen, hear, watch, see, receive, measure, discover

THE EFFECT OF YOUR ACTION IS UNPREDICTABLE

The precise consequences of action are always uncertain. No amount of planning and analysis can perfectly predict what will happen when we take action.

In her book *Changing Conversations in Organisations* Patricia Shaw puts it like this: note 24

> *Our interaction, no matter how considered or passionate, is always evolving in ways that we cannot control or predict in the longer term, no matter how sophisticated our planning tools.*

Since we cannot accurately predict the effects of our action, we must limit the time and energy we spend on trying to forecast the future, and focus our attention on noticing what is happening now. What happens may or may not be a direct result of your action. An organisation will never give you that satisfying sensation of being in total control. But it is possible to see progress towards a stated intention. So ask, always: What's happening now? Be attentive during your action.

We know we can potentially make a difference. But we can't know in advance of our action what exactly the difference is that we are going to make.

None of this should stop us from enthusiastically participating in action. But it should stop us from devoting too much time to detailed, exhaustive planning. We can divert that energy into attentive awareness, full participation and active response.

MAKE AWARENESS PART OF THE ACTION

In most change-management methodologies the 'measurement phase' of a change programme is separated from the action. Typically there is *note 25* a five-stage process or cycle:

1. *Analyse the status quo*
2. *Describe the goal or the problem*
3. *Plan*
4. *Make an intervention*
5. *Measure the benefit*

In my view, if you wait for the measurement phase, you've already left it too late. Get feedback immediately. Watch while you are doing, listen while you are speaking, collect data while you distribute information. Build the measurement into the action. Receive and transmit at the same time. Always ask: What's happening? What's next?

notes 26, 27

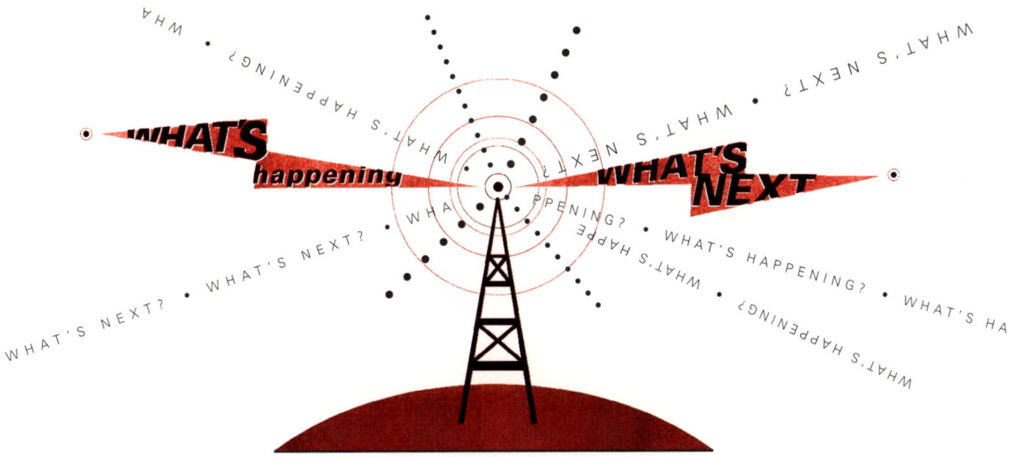

For example:

If you set up a team, notice the performance of that team, and also the performance of nearby teams. They may be encouraged by the new arrivals, or their resources may be drained to support the new initiative.

If you announce a forthcoming change:

- ask people what they heard you say;
- ask people what they think you are trying to achieve. You will, of course, have declared your intention – see Chapter 2. This is the time to check that your intentions have been heard, and not misconstrued;
- ask people what they think they are being asked to do differently;
- ask them if they will do anything differently as a result of this presentation.

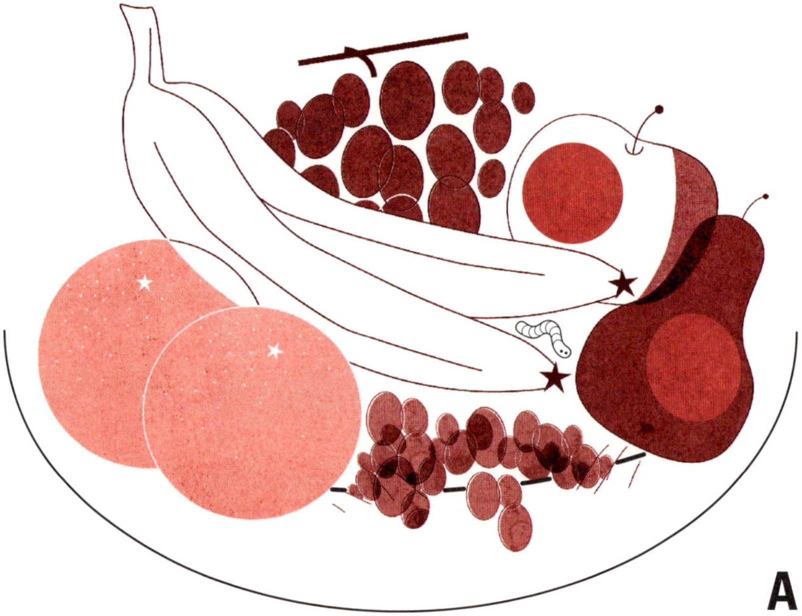

A

SPOT THE DIFFERENCE

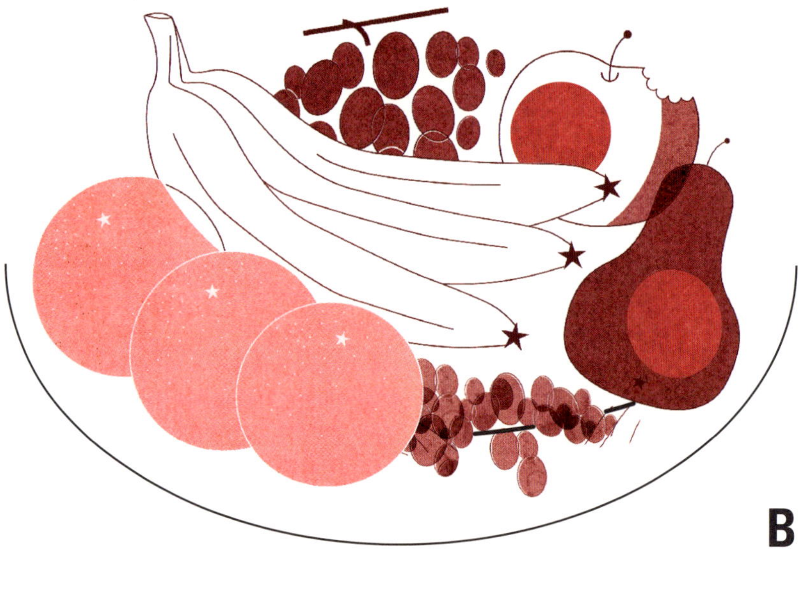

B

If you give a Health and Safety briefing, set a test at the end. In one safety-conscious corporation where I worked, your security pass was automatically disabled six weeks after joining, unless you had heard the Health and Safety Briefing and successfully completed the test. The test included such questions as 'What number do I dial for on-site emergency services?', 'Where is my assembly point?' and 'What do I do if I see an unattended package in the corridor?'

If you set up a system of milestone reports, go and investigate how they are being applied by projects. Visit project teams and see how the reports are used in practice. Who fills them in, using what information? What do they think will happen if they put 'Milestone Delayed' on the report?

The question is not

'Did I do my action?'

but

'Did I make a difference?'

You are interested in making change happen, not simply in ticking off a series of activities. Get real data, observations and information, from people affected by the change. Find out how your action has 'landed'.

Here's an example of how a consultant, Sheryl Nixon, is able to obtain an outcome by single-mindedly watching what's happening. In this cost-cutting example, Sheryl sees the details of how the cost is made up and watches only the results of the sub-projects. She isn't judging if managers are running a good sub-project or a bad one. She's not looking at activities on a plan. She's just looking at the total cost reduction, as of today. She is constantly asking 'Did we make a difference?' *note 28*

COST REDUCTION IN THE DEPARTMENT

Sheryl writes: 'We had to reduce costs. My client owned and operated the computers on the desks of a government department. The department had another supplier who provided a rather similar service a lot cheaper. So we had to do something to reduce our costs by about 40%. Then we could reduce our charges and still produce a profit. A result was needed within a matter of months.

'We did it by running a large number of initiatives which we called "reforms". Before we started, we set some rules. We were really clear on the outcome we wanted. We analysed the finances until we had every cost component of the desktop computer in a list. Then, any idea was welcome so long as someone could show that it was going to reduce the costs on our list, directly and in the short term. We ran brainstorming sessions which produced lots of ideas, and we selected only those which had a high probability of success and where we could calculate the effect they were going to have on the costs. So ideas like "Communicate the value of our service" were out – it's too indirect. Ideas like "Remove all unused equipment" were in. The person who proposed removing the unused equipment could show how much of it there was, what it was costing us, and therefore what the potential cost saving was.

'We maintained a "pipeline" of cost savings in progress, in the same way that a sales team maintains a pipeline of sales in progress. Our cost-saving opportunities were weighted by probability of success and we tracked the weighted totals very frequently – weekly or sometimes daily. If someone's opportunity was drifting downwards in weighted total, then we stopped that activity and diverted the effort to an opportunity which was going to have a bigger effect.

'On the management team, we didn't track progress on activities. We didn't ask for milestone charts or project plans. All we were interested in was the current predicted effect of that idea on costs.

> We just tracked the outcome. We had to be very single-minded because we had so little time. We managed to reach our target by this means, so the system worked. We passed the cost savings on to the department, and we kept their business.'

WHEN YOU'VE GOT LIMITED RESOURCES, MONITOR WHAT'S HAPPENING (OUTCOMES IN THE PRESENT) RATHER THAN MONITORING PROGRESS (ACTIVITIES IN THE PAST)

AWARENESS USES ALL THE SENSES TO MEASURE EFFECTS

An organisation is not mechanical. It is a group of people, interacting.

To act with awareness you have to be connected. You have to be there, with people. Don't just listen, hear; don't just watch, see. Ask questions and listen to the answers. Let the answers have an effect. In the cost-cutting example above, it would have been no good if Sheryl had done all the monitoring and then taken no action. She took action: when there was no progress with an idea, when it produced no improvement in the costs, it was abandoned and the effort re-allocated.

How do you assess 'the impact of doing things'? You stay connected. Use many channels of information, in particular the human ones. Use spreadsheets of data, but remember that these are just one of your sources of information. Use the experience and knowledge of people around you, and your skills of hearing and seeing. Let what you hear and see affect what you think and do. Practise the art of dialogue, which the author William Isaacs calls 'the art of thinking together'. For many people this means being in the office, and on the shopfloor, and out with customers. It means listening to a wide range of people and being influenced by what you hear and see. *note 29*

The following example from Sanderson shows how a manager stays connected.

NICK WALROND, MANAGING DIRECTOR OF SANDERSON PLC

NICK WALROND ASSESSES THE IMPACT OF CHANGE

'It's an open-plan office. I sit in the middle of the office. There are a hundred people, all around. I get a feel, a gut feel. You hear people talking to each other, what they say to customers, how they talk about customers. When there was a big change, like when we split administration and account management, then I made sure I talked to people about it directly. I pulled up a chair to their desk and talked to them where they were. Asked questions, listened to answers.

'Certain people were directly affected. I spent time with them. Like, one person, an account manager. I carry a senior relationship with customers. It was her account; we needed to visit the customer together. So we had a reason to talk. I used that opportunity to ask her about other things. We had a whole two and a half hours in the car. I'm talking directly to staff, to the people affected, not just through their manager. Their manager doesn't get upset. I'm talking to their staff about very specific things. The conversations are functional. In any case we have weekly management meetings where I'm talking with the managers. As well as that we monitor the financial figures. And other things, like absenteeism.'

DON'T JUST LISTEN, HEAR; DON'T JUST WATCH, SEE

ATTENTIVENESS IN ACTION: PRACTICAL APPLICATION

So here's the test:

- CHOOSE THE ACTION

  Are you sure those things in your diary and those actions on your To Do list are the most effective ways to turn your intentions into reality? Will they work? (See Chapter 4.)

- GET INTO ACTION

  If there's an action you are avoiding: what is it and how can you get yourself to do it? (See Chapter 5.)

- REMAIN ATTENTIVE

  For the actions you have scheduled, how are you going to remain attentive to what's happening? (See this chapter.)

  - If you are going to give a presentation, how will you discover what the audience heard? Will they act on what they heard?
  - If you are preparing to speak to someone, are you equally preparing to hear?
  - How will you notice and be influenced by the effects of what you are doing?

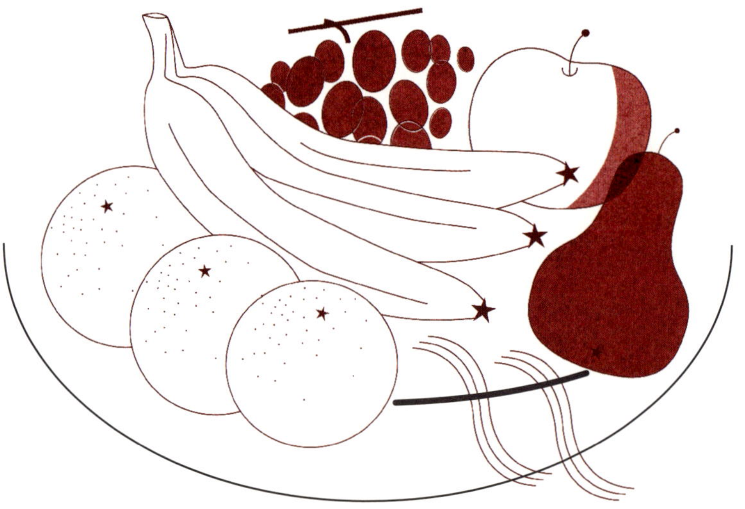

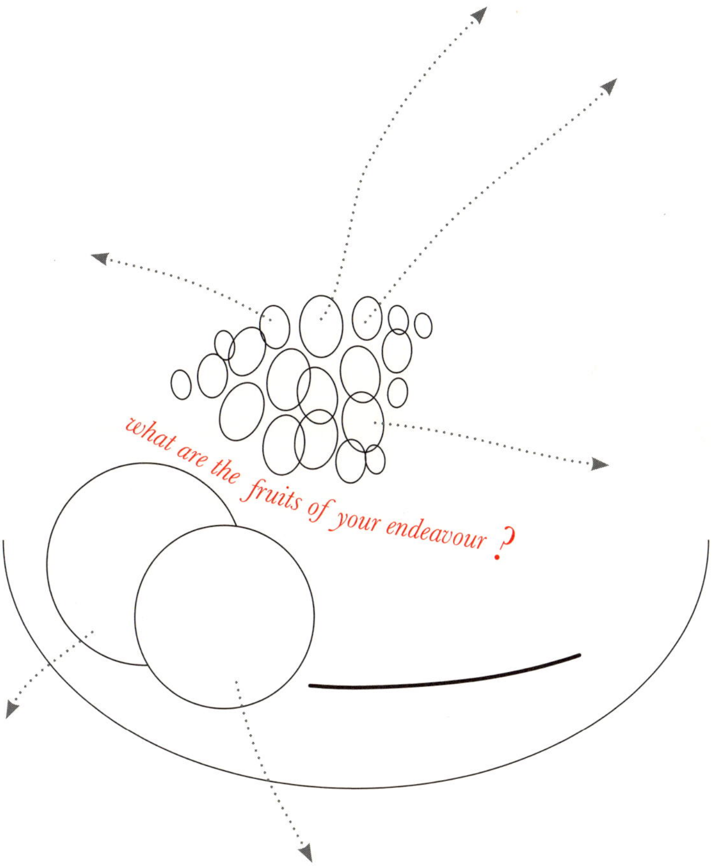
what are the fruits of your endeavour ?

7 CONTINUE

We have examined how to declare an intention, and how to state the change you want. The previous chapter considered how to get into action and emphasised the importance of attentiveness while in action.

In this chapter we consider how to continue the progress, using the information and experience you gain from action.

The messages in this chapter are:

- use the results you see to inform changes in your intentions and your actions
- as soon as something starts happening, then new options are possible

WHAT SHALL I DO WITH WHAT I'VE DONE?

Once we start to achieve something of what we want, there are always a number of options for how to make progress. These are set out below. I use as an example 'Omar', whose intention was to reduce the number of calls to the help desk.

The help desk agents were swamped with calls. Users were irate at not getting through. Omar headed a short-term call-reduction programme. He intended to reduce the number of calls per day down to a target level, which was defined in his project initiation document. He succeeded. One measure which worked was to equip users to reset their own passwords so they didn't have to call the help desk every time they forgot what password they had chosen. There were about a dozen more measures, including, for example, getting automatic messages put on the phone lines during planned outages, so users didn't take up agents' time when the cause of their problem was known.

Having reduced the call volume down to manageable levels, what should Omar do with what he's done?

WHAT SHALL I DO WITH WHAT I'VE DONE?

having changed something, WHAT NEXT?	EXAMPLE
Embed it Make sure it doesn't revert to how it was before	We don't want the call volumes to go up again the moment Omar stops his active campaign. So, for example, Omar can get his automatic messages incorporated into the standard procedures for planned maintenance, and included in audit checks, so they become part of the way we do business, and he can be sure they won't get forgotten.
Reframe it View this change as progress towards something different	Having established the principle that users can reset their own passwords, perhaps this could be regarded as progress towards a new strategy of user self-service. The next action in this new strategy might be to get users to order their own equipment from a catalogue.
Enlarge it Address bigger or more far-reaching opportunities	Having addressed the immediate overload, Omar could address wider issues: • Why are we getting so many systems failures in the first place? • Why do people keep forgetting their passwords? He could improve the quality of call handling in the help desk so there are fewer repeat calls.
Repeat it Do it again	Omar could apply the same successful interventions to other help desks and other service desks in the company.
Extend it Go further, have a bigger effect	He might be able to take more actions to reduce call volumes further.
Generalise it Create the process for doing what you did	Omar's experiences might be of general benefit in the company: he could create a training course or methodology and use it to help others do what he's done.

Each of these options is 'progress', and each inspires its own set of further intentions, related to Omar's original. Each is aligned with different overall business strategies.

Below I consider the first two of these in greater depth: embed, and reframe.

EMBEDDING THE CHANGE

note 30

© Ashleigh Brilliant www.ashleighbrilliant.com

By 'embedding the change' we mean 'making the change stick'. We want our new way of doing things to become part of the way people habitually operate. Here are some ways to do that:

- get your change into the corporate processes
- tell people what's happening and why
- encourage traditions, conventions and behaviours which reinforce the change
- keep your intention clear

These are each considered further below.

Get your change into the corporate processes

If you want your change to last, then you must pay attention to all those systems and processes in an organisation that exist to preserve the status quo. Get your change incorporated into those systems and processes. All of those processes are surrounded by communication and governance mechanisms: manuals, training, newsletters, reports, business management meetings. All of such mechanisms become the vehicle for embedding your change.

The most powerful of those processes is the budgeting process, or whatever the equivalent is where you work. The next most powerful is the performance management process. If you can get your change incorporated into these processes and their communication mechanisms, it will stay in place.

In Omar's company the budgeting process took the form of an annual planning cycle. To make his change endure, Omar got businesses to budget for the equipment upgrade that enabled users securely to change their own passwords including the training and the communication programmes.

Call volumes had been a performance measure of the help desk. Omar collected call volume data by location and business unit too. By communicating this through management meetings he was able to draw attention to specific locations where high call volumes indicated that user training was needed. Call volumes became a shared performance measure between the help desk and the business.

Ultimately, to make sure his changes were not immediately reversed, Omar had to take action in areas far from the help desk. For example, he had to get the processes for planned maintenance changed. He made it part of their mandatory procedure that they arranged for automated messages to go on the help desk phone line. This extra step had to be built into company procedure, and included in the audit programme.

Tell people what's happening, and why. Get their ideas

Use the organisation's formal and informal networks to send and receive news of your change.

In the case of Omar's help desk, his process changes were accomplished by using manuals, courses, presentations and events. These communicated what was changing and why the changes were necessary. People contributed their further ideas on how to reduce call volumes.

Encourage traditions, conventions and behaviours which reinforce the change

Omar's actions gradually changed the way people regarded the help desk. This was a cultural change. 'Culture', as used here, means 'the messages we receive about how we are expected to behave around here'. People had regarded the help desk as an infinite free resource, a final dumping ground for problems and complications which could not be sorted out elsewhere. By making cost and usage data available, and putting a clear limit on call volumes, Omar made people include the help desk in their plans and calculations. These explicit changes had a more subtle, indirect, effect. New, unspoken, conventions were established which guided people on what was, and what was not, a valid reason for calling the help desk. A certain level of self-sufficiency became established as a value. These cultural changes contributed to reducing the call volumes to a level where they could be managed.

note 31

Such cultural changes come about as a result of the visible changes that people like Omar put in place. You can't legislate for 'self-sufficiency', but you can notice it happening, notice that it helps the change you are trying to accomplish, and encourage it in conversations, meetings and communications.

Keep your intention clear

While making these changes, though remote from the help desk itself, Omar still had the same end in view: he was still reducing call volumes.

In many change initiatives, however, the intention changes. We'll have a look at this now.

REFRAMING THE CHANGE: THE PROGRESS CATWALK

The classic model of business change describes linear progress towards a fixed goal. *note 32*

[*linear progress towards a fixed goal*]

This model is useful for certain sorts of engineering projects, office moves, and computer systems installations and upgrades.

In many cases this classic model does not match what happens. Once we get into action we see a range of options for possible future directions. These options were invisible when we started. We are not making single-minded progress towards a fixed goal, but moving, open-minded, towards chosen possibilities as they present themselves. The skill here is to have a clear, stated intention, to take decisive action in the stated direction, and to pay attention to what happens so that you remain alive to new possibilities and can restate your intention.

The classic programme management model has governance structures which are designed to discourage a change of intention. Such changes, where they occur, must undergo such onerous procedures that they are often disguised or hidden.

An alternative model of business change describes constant adaptation of direction.

[remain alive to new possibilities, restate your intention]

We need to be able to use a model where the end goal is not fixed, and the steps are not linear, and where it is permissible to change direction. We will always have a clear intention, we may always have a goal in view, and we certainly always have a plan, but none of these is static. Instead of progress in a straight line towards a fixed goal, we have a series of unfolding scenarios. In this real world, we do not want a governance structure which is designed to keep things fixed. We need governance designed to ensure action is rigorously aligned with the current intention. We need mechanisms to change the intention, clearly and decisively, as the change unfolds.

The following story illustrates the steps described in the previous chapters, and shows how new possibilities are revealed as change happens.

SECURING THE FUTURE: NIGEL AND UNITY

Nigel Phillipps's clear intention when we met in February 2007 was to provide a secure future for his company, Unity, and remove uncertainty. One of their clients is Somerfield, the UK supermarket chain. Nigel was determined to form a stronger relationship with Somerfield, to provide continuity of income for his company. Somerfield had another software supplier, based in Bangalore in India. This other supplier could provide services at low cost. This Indian software supplier sometimes won projects, and Unity sometimes won projects. Unity could not compete with the Indian supplier on cost. Cost was often a deciding criterion, so the future business for Unity looked uncertain.

STEP 1
declare your intention

note 33

'We decided to go "up the value chain",' said Nigel. 'I'd heard this expression, but it took me a while to work out what it meant for us in practice. In our case it meant that we had to become the first people Somerfield called when they were thinking about a project. We wanted to be there at the beginning.'

STEP 2
describe the change: from and to

from [*today*]	*to* [*future*]
They call us when they know what they want: they have developed the business case and the project Terms of Reference.	They talk to us before they know what they want. We get involved early: we are engaged with the business when they first have a problem to solve.

STEP 3

choose effective action: direct action, make a request

STEP 4

get into action: do it without delay

STEP 5

be aware: monitor the outcome, listen to others

'We put this proposal to Somerfield: we asked them to use us as their design authority. We had the expert knowledge of their systems and we knew the market, so we could help their business people take the right choices about what to develop. Two months after approaching them, they accepted our offer. Their businesses have a wish list and a budget. We help them generate the business cases and the terms of reference for projects. Because we work across all the business functions, we can often see how to put several projects together, which saves them money. They love that. We've gone from not being involved in the decision-making to being instrumental. The Indian software company still gets the work that they excel at: the building and operation of the systems. We've stayed in dialogue with them and come to a good agreement.

'We now have a clear role within Somerfield and steady work. We have a commitment from them to use our services.'

The change happened.

STEP 6

continue: reframe the change

Nigel is still working through the implications of this change for his company. He sees a number of possibilities which it has opened up. Unity can position themselves as design authority for other clients. This might be a new line of business. They could use the security that the updated contract provides to develop new services and product offerings. They now have a number of options which they could not previously have envisaged.

Nigel says, 'I would have been perfectly happy to "secure the future" with Somerfield in any number of ways. We did it this way, and so now we have to decide where we want that to take us next.'

AS CHANGE HAPPENS, NEW POSSIBILITIES EMERGE

WHAT NEXT?

In my view, the work of business change is one of constantly having a stated intention, and working towards it with vigour and decisiveness, while remaining aware that this very progress will provoke you to revise what it is you are trying to achieve.

The succession of possibilities is continuous and endless, and can be confusing. It's always possible to state a direction, even if it's not always possible to describe a goal.

So, as you continue to make change happen:

- *Ask* 'What shall I do with what I've done?';
- *Decide* to keep your intention the same or to change it;
- *Restate* your intention frequently, especially when it changes.

ASK

DECIDE

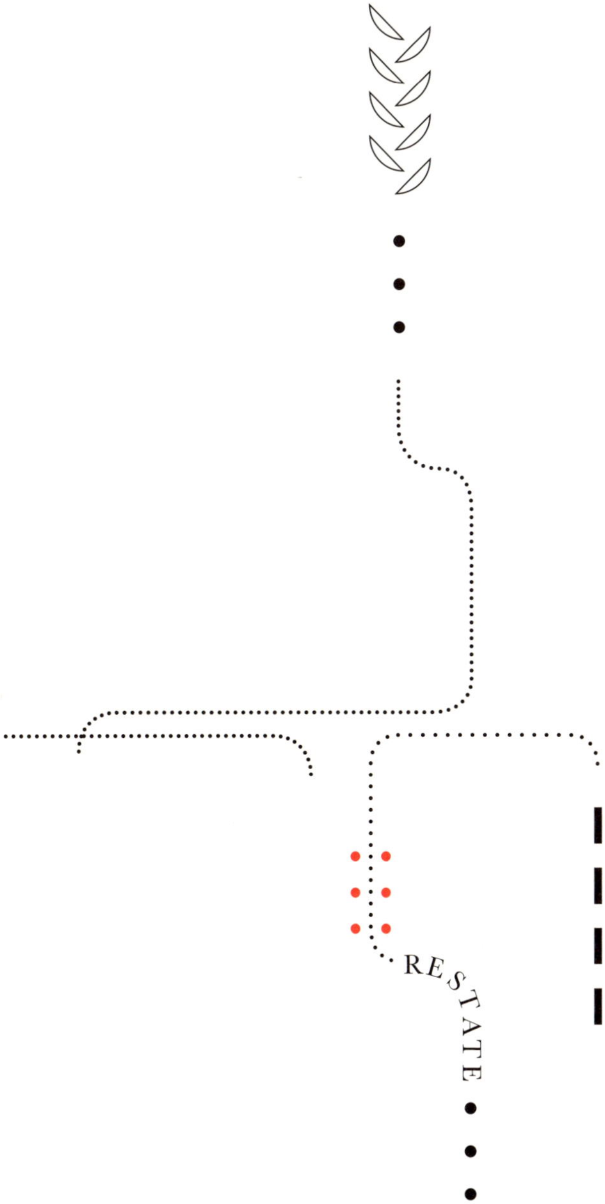
RESTATE

8 CONVERSATIONS THAT WORK

This chapter and the next present some techniques for making change happen. This chapter provides practical suggestions for how to get things done in conversations. The following chapter looks at how to get action to happen in meetings.

At work we spend a lot of time in conversations. This chapter offers some techniques for how to use conversations as powerful vehicles for action. This is a large subject. Here I describe just a few of the techniques and ways of thinking I have found useful. Further reading is in the Notes.

The messages in this chapter are:

- conversation is a tool for getting things done
- the way to get someone to do something is to ask

THERE ARE DIFFERENT TYPES OF CONVERSATIONS

Change in business is accomplished through conversation: listening and speaking with other people.

Conversation is a skill: by becoming aware of different ways of speaking and listening we can become more skilled at making change happen. *note 34*

There are a number of different types of conversation. On the next page are some common types in use in business.

COMMON TYPES OF CONVERSATION IN BUSINESS

INFORMative

TO EXCHANGE FACTS, EXPERIENCES, FEEDBACK

DEBATE

TO ESTABLISH POINTS OF VIEW,
EXPLORE OPTIONS

RANT!

RANT FOR SELF-EXPRESSION,
TO GIVE VENT TO ANGER,
EXASPERATION, FRUSTRATION

ACTION

TO GET SOMETHING TO HAPPEN

There are many others. There are conversations to establish status or superiority, to persuade, encourage or praise. There are flirtations, sales conversations, and conversations for pure entertainment and pleasure.

Here I will focus on conversations for action. These are specific business conversations whose purpose is to get something to happen. They don't always work. If we want to make change happen we need to notice what works and enhance our skill in this type of conversation. Conversation is a tool for making things happen. We can learn how to make better use of it. Here's my experience.

What works: asking someone to do something

If you want to initiate action, you must ask someone to do something. When you use a conversation to make action happen you think:

- What will I ask for?
- What am I offering to do?
- What I am listening for?

During the conversation remember to keep asking yourself:

- Did I ask, and was I heard? What was the reply?
- Did I make my offer? Was it accepted?
- Did I hear? And did I hear correctly?

The only way to be sure that you have initiated action is to ask someone to do something, and to hear the response. They may say 'No'. In this case you can ask someone else, or find out from them what they can do.

They may say 'Yes'. If you get a definite 'Yes', then action is likely: someone is committed to the task.

Of course they may say 'Yes' and still do nothing. But in general the thing that causes us to be let down is our own failure to ask, or our failure to hear the response. If you don't ask, you won't get. Increase the probability of action happening by asking, and by hearing the answer. Make sure you get a definite 'Yes' or 'No'.

Making a request

Here's a basic way to make a request:

- Declare your intention
  'I'm trying to make some space so we can use this area to create a prototype customer service facility.'
- Make a request for someone to do something:
  'Andrew, can you please find out how much it would cost to put all this equipment in storage for two months?'
- Specify a time:
  'I need to know by 5pm tomorrow, so I can get the business case approved by Mike on Friday.'
- Give them the option to say 'No':
  'Is tomorrow realistic – can you do it?'
- Hear the response:
  'Yes, I'll call some suppliers. I'll also find out if there's any storage space on site. You mean you want to clear out all the stuff that's in this office and in the corridor? I'll find out the removal costs as well.'
- Confirm what you've heard:
  'Yes, exactly, this office and that corridor. A couple of supplier quotes for removal and storage would be perfect, in writing, if possible.'

There are plenty of other ways of asking for the action. My point here is not to set out a formula so much as to draw attention to the details of how we make requests and listen to responses. These details make a difference to whether action occurs or not.

You must hear the response to your request. Communication breaks down, and change fails to happen, when we ask for action and the person says 'No' but we hear 'Yes'. This phenomenon is explored further below.

Hearing 'No'

There are many ways to say *'No'*. Misunderstanding and inaction occur when people say *'No'* and we hear *'Yes'*.

Here are ways someone could say *'No'* but you might hear *'Yes'*.

WHAT THEY SAY:	WHAT THEY MEAN:
'I'll look into it.'	*'. . . if I have time.'*
'I'll do my best.'	*'. . . but I may not be able to fit it in.'*
'No problem.'	*'. . . in principle, but this is item 53 on my list and I've not agreed to do it.'*
'I'll consider it.'	*'. . . but I won't necessarily do it.'*
'I'll see if Frank has time to do it.'	*'. . . and if he hasn't then this request will go nowhere.'*
'I'll see what I can do'	*'. . . and I may not do anything.'*

What we are looking for is a 'Yes'. We are looking for a response like this:

'Yes, I will. I'll do it this afternoon and give you an answer tomorrow morning.'

Only now is action likely to happen.

'No' is also a useful response. It means we must modify our request, or go and ask someone else. 'No' is a good answer and helps the action. When we ask someone to do something we must be ready to hear the answer 'No' and we must accept it as a valid response. If someone says 'No' and we hear 'No' then we have to try something else. We can keep moving.

It is misunderstanding which frustrates action. The answer 'No' is useful: make sure you hear it.

WHAT DOESN'T WORK: HOPING THEY'LL GUESS WHAT YOU MEAN

In the section above I described *requests*. It is important to distinguish requests from other types of conversation which are useful but which may not work to drive action.

Here's what tends to happen unless we are alert. We describe a current injustice in the expenses system. The person from Human Resources agrees that it is a problem. Since it's clearly a Human Resources issue, we think she'll take it away and fix it. She thinks that we are describing an issue we are going to escalate through our line management for resolution. Neither of us takes any action. The expenses system is going to stay the same. Nothing will change.

This conversation fails to produce action because all we have done is describe a problem. To produce action we must say to the Human Resources person something like: 'To sort out this inequality, please could you arrange that my engineers are reimbursed on the same terms as the sales people?' We have now asked for action, and the Human Resources person knows what she has to do.

Don't just describe a problem: ask for action.

CONVERSATIONS THAT DON'T DRIVE ACTION

Many conversations have no action agenda. They are useful for information exchange, self-expression or relationship building. Recognise these conversations, and note that if you want to produce action, you will need to shift the conversation and make a request, or offer to do something.

Here are some conversations which you will need to shift if you want action to happen:

- Describing a wish:
  'The product line we want has five components . . .'

- Explaining a problem:
  'The difficulty with the current sales situation is that the sales force is largely technical, and so . . .'

- Self-expression:
  'I am upset that he . . .'

- Narrating a history:
  'The supplier was near to bankruptcy, and so we . . .'

- Asking questions:
  'How much time do we have?'
  'How many people are there who know how this system works?'

- Giving information:
  'Paul has a list of cost codes.'
  'Here is the organisation chart for . . .'
  'The email system is supplied by . . .'

- Complaining:
  'Nobody seems to be taking my proposal seriously. I get pushed from pillar to post. The engineering manager is always on leave and I . . .'

These are important precursors to action. They might build relationships which lead to action and, indeed, someone might do something as a result of these conversations. But they might lead to action, and they might not. You can't tell whether they will or not.

If you want action move to a different conversation, such as one of those set out below.

HOW TO USE CONVERSATIONS TO DRIVE ACTION

Ask someone to do something:

'Please could you: . . .'

Obtain a commitment from someone to do something:

'That's agreed then.
So you'll do this: . . .'

Offer to do something or promise to do it:

'I'll do this: . . .'

Always make sure you hear the response: be ready to hear *'Yes'* or *'No'*.

ASK *yes?*

no.

[request]

[response]

9 MEETINGS WHERE CHANGE HAPPENS

In the previous chapter we looked at how the detailed exchanges between people in conversation can contribute to making things happen.

This chapter considers how to get action to happen in meetings. Meetings are long conversations between a number of people. We'll look at some ways to structure meetings in order to get action to happen.

The messages in this chapter are:

- a default assumption is that a meeting generates a list of 'things to be done' (actions) and the action occurs after the meeting
- it's possible to get action to happen in the meeting
- a meeting in which action happens is exciting and powerful

CHANGE CAN HAPPEN IN THE MEETING

We've all been at meetings where something has actually happened. We agreed the basis of collaboration, we signed a contract, we set our budgets. In such meetings we have a sense of achievement. There is progress and, importantly, we have made progress together as a group. We have shared an experience.

Meetings usually generate 'action lists': somebody 'takes an action' to do after the meeting.

It's always worth asking the question:

> *'Instead of simply having actions from the meeting,*
> *can we have actions in the meeting?'*

Actions from meetings are usually regarded as boring and necessary.
note 35 Action in the meeting is much more interesting.

My purpose in this chapter is to draw attention to the possibility of action happening in the meeting, rather than afterwards. If you can get a business change to occur in the meeting, then you make progress rapidly. We've already seen the example of the 'Action Lab' on page 68 in Chapter 4.

Here is another example.

PROJECT INITIATION PANEL

> To their immense relief, a bid team had just won a large government contract, after months of laborious negotiations. Now the project team was ready to start on the engineering work to fulfil the contract. At this point, company procedure dictated that a 'Project Initiation Panel' ('PIP') was convened. The purpose was to inform the project team about the contract, so they could get started. This was also the point at which formal responsibility passed from the bid team to the project team. These PIP meetings were generally regarded as boring. The bid team was required to go through the contract in detail. The project team sat and listened. Quality-assurance people minuted that the meeting had happened. The contract moved to Stage 3. That was the procedure.
>
> Since this was a high-profile project with many people involved, the business unit manager wanted to be certain that the transition to the project team was accomplished effectively, with no doubts, no loose ends and no misunderstanding.
>
> Here's how we made action happen in the meeting to achieve his aim.

We made the transition from the bid team to the project team visible and public. The negotiator from the bid team brought the contract document: all six lever-arch files of it. These were shown to the assembled group at the beginning of the meeting. At the end of the meeting, to much applause, they were to be handed over to the commercial manager of the project team. This was a public, symbolic and physical act, which showed everyone what was happening.

However, before that handover could occur, the commercial team and the project manager wanted to be sure that the project team were ready to take on the work. So we resolved that not only were the contract sections to be presented to the project team, but the project team were going to be tested on its key points, during the meeting. The presenters could then check they had been heard and understood. Note that the purpose of the test was not to evaluate the listeners, but to give feedback to the speakers.

This certainly livened up the meeting. There were the inevitable presentations on overhead slides. But, every 20 minutes or so, the presenters stopped and distributed quiz sheets. They obtained immediate feedback by going through the answers. Sometimes everyone had misunderstood. Sometimes a single person had missed an important point, and so was rapidly put right by everyone else in the room. Sometimes the communication had been gratifyingly effective and everyone got all the answers right.

At the end, the project commercial manager asked everyone if they were ready for him to accept this large contractual commitment, represented by the heavy heap of files. They each gave him their consent and he ceremonially accepted the burden from the bid manager.

Change happened in that meeting. The project team took on responsibility for the contract. In the process, they learned together and helped each other learn as a group. The transfer of the responsibility was thus not simply from one individual to another, but from one group to another.

It was also, as one of them said, a lot more fun than just sitting listening to boring presentations.

MAKE CHANGE HAPPEN IN THE MEETING

Here are some ways of making change happen in a meeting:

Don't just decide: do

If the purpose is *to take a decision whether to do X*, consider making the purpose of the meeting *to take a decision whether to do X, and if the answer is 'Yes', to do it.*

Get customers in the room

For an annual planning meeting, it's possible to create the plan in the room, and at 5pm have some customers arrive. Tell them what you plan to do. Get their response and incorporate it into the plan on day two. Then you've not only created a plan in the abstract, but you've got some real-world acceptance.

Get decision-makers in the room

If you are designing some changes to operational processes, get the people in charge of those processes to arrive at midday to approve the changes. In the afternoon, start work making changes.

Create the work product together in the room

Instead of simply discussing a service concept, create a marketing brochure or website for the service, using professional designers and artists. These people work amazingly quickly, and can produce visible products during the meeting. These can be used as the basis for communicating the results of the meeting. These communications form the basis of more polished products later.

Call up help here and now

If you have a meeting to solve a problem, set it up so that specialist advisers or approvers know that the meeting is taking place and are available on the phone. They don't need to be at the meeting but they need to be available to answer specific questions. Too often, action in meetings is frustrated because we can't find Mark, who is the only one who can give permission to bring the security patching cycle forwards by a week. Before the meeting, think: If we want to take this action forwards in the meeting, who might we want to consult? Tell them they might be consulted. Get them to appoint a deputy. Usually, people can step out of another activity to answer your specific question or give approval for a course of action, even when they cannot dedicate the whole morning to come to your meeting. By this means you can not only agree to implement a solution, but also use the meeting to start the implementation.

Do the financial calculations in the room

Sometimes a meeting can't make progress because someone has to 'go away and work the numbers'. As an alternative, consider asking an imaginative accountant to create skeleton financial models in advance of the meeting, and to populate them as people develop options during the discussions. This informs the conversations in the room, so that you get immediate feedback on the financial implications of suggestions. Then it's possible to take informed decisions in the meeting without delay.

Do individual work together

Typically, people meet in a room to take a decision, then go away to do their individual actions. Sometimes it's useful to keep people together while they do their individual actions. This sustains the momentum, provides peer pressure to make sure the actions get done, and gives the group a sense of achievement. It also gives people the opportunity to get immediate feedback from their colleagues on their work.

Measure progress during the meeting

Invent a way of measuring the change that's happening during your meeting. A business unit managing director was worried that her managers were consumed by operational matters, and neglecting the growth targets. She convened a meeting to impress on them the importance of growth. She wanted to use the knowledge of the group to uncover new opportunities and co-ordinate action on existing sales. Her intention was that the managers would see the need for growth, and would know what to do to get it. So we measured where people were on those two criteria during the meeting, by using a Dot Chart. This tool has the dual purpose of clearly informing participants about the expected outcomes of the meeting, and giving them an anonymous vote on progress. This is useful information for the person leading the meeting.

The purpose of the Dot Chart is to measure the changes that occur during the meeting. Participants anonymously put dots on the chart to indicate 'where I am right now'. This 'temperature check' is taken two or three times during the meeting, and used to influence the meeting content.

Use intervals for action

Instead of a two-hour continuous meeting, consider a half-hour meeting in which the group decides what to do, then a one-hour interval in which they do it, individually or in small groups. After the 'interval for action' there is another half-hour meeting to confirm what's been done, and to determine what's next.

Meetings for action – it's an attitude of mind

None of these techniques is a formula for success. The key is to think of meetings as part of a process:

- What is the process of which this meeting is a part?
- Can we get more of that process done in this meeting?

So consider:

- rather than just deciding, can we decide *and do*?
- instead of just discussing it, can we *try it*?
- instead of listing the actions, can we *do the actions*?
- what is the change we want, and can we *make it happen in the room*?
- if we can make it happen, can we *measure it happening*?

MEETING ROOM *IN USE*

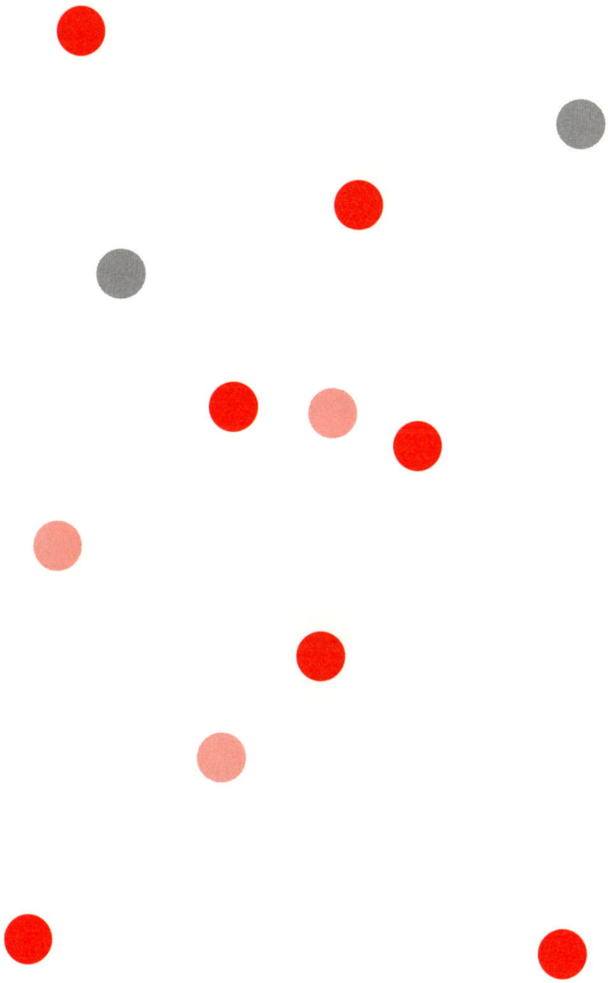

CONCLUSION

The important thing to keep in mind is that models are only models and that all of physics need not be described in terms of a single model.

• *Eyvind H. Wichmann* *note 36*

A theme of this book is that it is action, not dreams or ideas, that makes a difference in business. Taking action, however limited in extent, is preferable to expending endless energy on grand plans which go nowhere. The business world I experience is pragmatic. If something works, then let's do it – the theory can come later.

It seems to me important that actions are intentional. As responsible adults, we must be able to account for our actions. We must know what consequences we expect from our actions, and take responsibility for those consequences. Aligning actions with intentions is a principle underlying my consulting practice, and it is central to the discussions in this book.

I hope you have found this book useful. I want to emphasise that I've described *a* way, not *the* way. As Wichmann says above: 'all of physics need not be described in terms of a single model'. Likewise, there are many valid models for addressing change. This is my contribution.

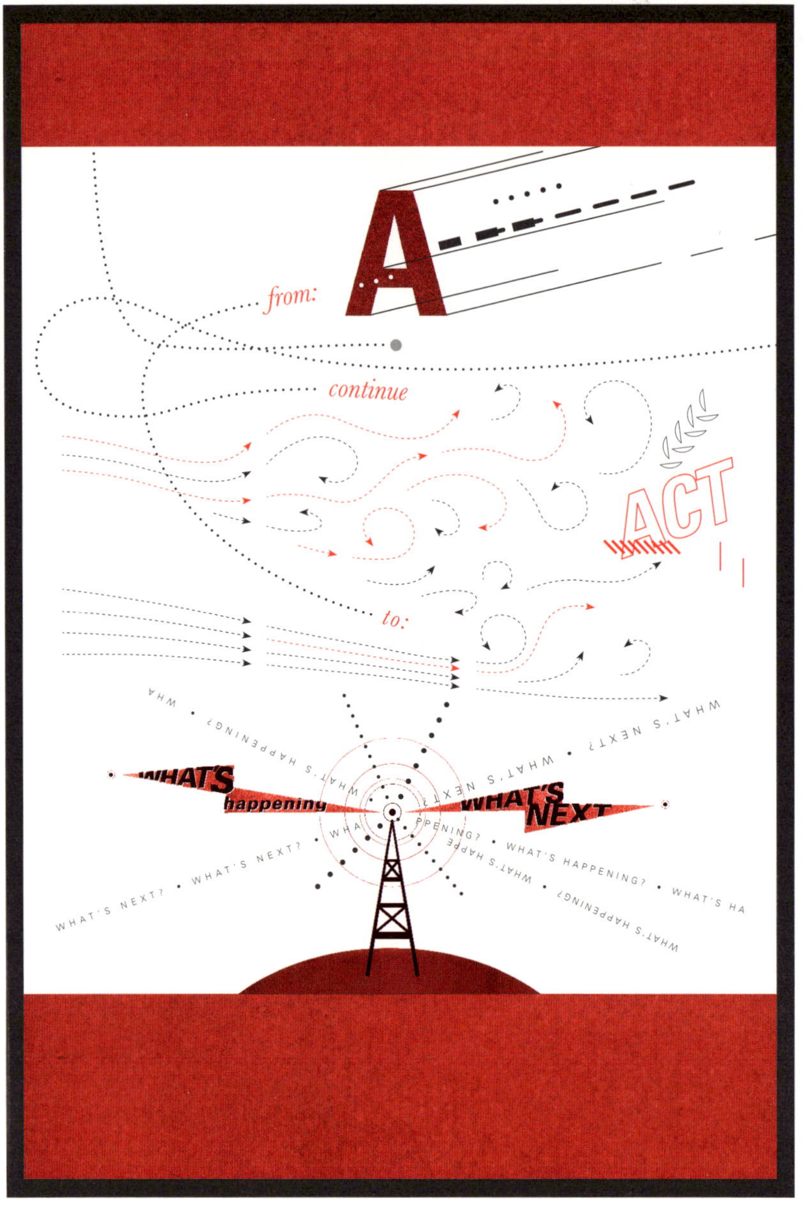
A
from:
continue
ACT
to:
WHAT'S
happening
WHAT'S
NEXT
WHAT'S NEXT? • WHAT'S NEXT?
WHAT'S HAPPENING? • WHAT'S HA
WHAT'S HAPPENING?

A BASIC METHOD FOR ACTION-ORIENTED CHANGE

STEP 1 *Declare your intention*
WHAT AM I TRYING TO ACHIEVE?

STEP 2 *Describe the change you want in terms of from and to*
WHAT DIFFERENCE WILL IT MAKE?

STEP 3 *Choose effective action*
WHAT SHALL I DO?

STEP 4 *Get into action*
DO IT!

STEP 5 *Be aware*
WHAT'S HAPPENING?

STEP 6 *Continue*
WHAT'S NEXT?

If you want someone to do something, ask them, and hear the response.

If you convene a meeting, use it to make something happen.

You can change the course of history.

MAKE CHANGE HAPPEN.

NOTES

FRONTISPIECE

1 The poem 'What if this road' by Sheenagh Pugh comes from her collection *Id's Hospit* and is reproduced by kind permission of the author. Published by Seren, Poetry Wales Press, First Floor, 2 Wyndham Street, Bridgend, Wales (1997).

INTRODUCTION

2 *The implementation stage of a project, the part where action happens*

See Theodore Levitt, 'Creativity is not Enough' in *Harvard Business Review* (HBR) 1963 classic reprint R0208K, and also reproduced in HBR OnPoint collection: 'Best of HBR on Innovation: One Part Inspiration, Two Parts Discipline', 1 August 2002. Theodore Levitt gives examples of ideas which come to nothing because there is no follow-through. He advocates that a manager instil 'Responsible Creativity' as an antidote to this. Managers should insist that innovators think through the implementation plan of their great idea.

3 *Change at the level of the corporation*

For a comprehensive review, see Richard Lynch, *Corporate Strategy* (4th edition), Prentice Hall and the *Financial Times* (2005). This gives an overview of strategic models and theories of strategy and also describes various models for implementing strategy.

4 *Step-by-step change methods*

John Kotter describes an 8-step process for achieving broad-based major change driven by strategy and vision in *Leading Change*, Harvard Business School Press (1996), ISBN 0-87584-747-1.

For problem-solving and process improvement programmes, see for example the Six Sigma process, which offers a five-step process: DMAIC (Define–Measure–Analyse–Improve–Control). This is described in *What is Six Sigma?* by Pete Pande and Larry Holpp, McGraw Hill (2002).

These processes describe project stages undertaken by a team to tackle large-scale change. The process I describe focuses primarily on the journey of an individual taking action locally.

For holistic change frameworks at the corporate level see, for example, Michael Hammer and James Champy, *Reengineering the Corporation: A Manifesto for Business Revolution*, HarperCollins Publishers (1993), ISBN 0-88730-640-3. Their 'Business System Diamond' holistic change framework is in Chapter 4.

Another example of a corporate-level holistic change framework is the 7-S model used to analyse 'As Is' and 'To Be' states in an organisation. There is a succinct description of this and other frameworks in Steven ten Have, Wouter ten Have, Frans Stevens and Marcel van der Elst with Fiona Pol-Coyne, *Key Management Models*, FT Prentice Hall and Pearson Education Ltd (2002), ISBN 978-0-273-66201-3.

CHAPTER 1: MAKING CHANGE HAPPEN

5 *Small changes are significant*

If you are leading a change, the co-ordinated action of many individuals is necessary to produce the effect you are aiming for. Equally, local individual action can under certain circumstances produce step-change and a new equilibrium, whether or not the local individual intended it so. There does not need to be a master plan or a 'change leader' to orchestrate such a shift. Examples of this emergent order abound in nature and human society and are described in a fascinating book, *Critical Mass*, by Philip Ball. Ball describes how cultures of bacteria will take on orderly patterns without, as he puts it, a 'Master Bacterium dictating their movements'. Philip Ball, *Critical Mass – how one thing leads to another*, Arrow Books, The Random House Group Limited (2005), ISBN 978-0-099-45786-2.

Other books on emergent order and self-organising systems are: Ralph Stacey, Douglas Griffin and Patricia Shaw, *Complexity and Management*, Routledge (2000), ISBN 0-415-24761-6; and Richard T. Pascale, Mark Milleman and Linda Gioja, *Surfing the Edge of Chaos*, Three Rivers Press (CA) (2001), ISBN 0-609-80883-4.

CHAPTER 2: DECLARE YOUR INTENTION

6 *Vision: creating and using a vision*

For a description of 'Vision' see Chapter 5 of *Leading Change* by John P. Kotter (see note 4). For a great story illustrating that visioning doesn't help when you are in a crisis, see 'Step 1: When Alligators are nipping at your heels' in Kotter's *The Heart of Change*, Harvard Business School Publishing (2002), ISBN 1-57851-254-9. The same book has several examples of useful Visions in Step 3.

7 *Questions to reveal intention*

Books on coaching contain questions which help reveal intention. See, for example, Laura Whitworth, Henry Kimsey-House and Phil Sandhal, *Co-active Coaching*, Davies Black Publishing (1998), ISBN 0-89106-123-1.

CHAPTER 3: DESCRIBE THE CHANGE

8 *SMART objectives*

Opinions vary over the definitions of the letters in SMART:
A sometimes stands for Attainable;
R sometimes stands for Relevant or Realistic;
T sometimes stands for Target Date.

9 Sanderson, www.sandersonplc.com, Clifton Down House, 54 Whiteladies Road, Clifton, Bristol, UK, BS8 3NH, tel: + 44 (0)117 970 6666.

10 *Keeping what's good*

Appreciative Inquiry is a philosophy of change which places emphasis on keeping what's good. If we do more of what works, it 'crowds out' what doesn't work. See, for example, Sue Annis Hammond, *The Thin Book of Appreciative Inquiry* (2nd edition), Thin Book Publishing Company, PO Box 260608, Plano, TX 75026-0608 USA (1998). www.thinbook.com

11 There are two St Clement churches in the city of London. The one in Eastcheap no longer plays the 'Oranges and Lemons' tune, but St Clement Danes in the Strand does.

CHAPTER 4: CHOOSE EFFECTIVE ACTION

12 *Choosing what to do*

Five Frogs on a Log describes the use of 'Value Driver Analysis' with respect to deciding which actions to take. See 'an exercise in establishing the relative value of alternative actions' on p. 50. Mark L. Feldman and Michael F. Spratt, *Five Frogs on a Log – A CEO's Guide to Accelerating the Transition in Mergers, Acquisitions, and Gut Wrenching Change,* John Wiley and Sons Ltd (1999), ISBN 0-471-98823-5.

13 Hôtel Jean-Jacques Rousseau, Rue Rousseau 13, 1201 Geneva, Switzerland. email: welcome@hotelrousseau.com, tel: +44 22 731 55 70.

14 *Taking direct action, not indirect action*

This principle is particularly important when applied to communicating information. Get your information, question or instruction delivered as closely as possible to the people to whom it's addressed. And get the answer back unfiltered. Information that has passed through more than one pair of hands becomes diluted and incoherent. If your change requires action at the operational level, then you'll need to be in direct face-to-face contact with the supervisor level: the people who manage the front-line staff. Cascade mechanisms are too indirect, they don't work. Larkin and Larkin are very persuasive on this point: T. J. Larkin and Sandar Larkin, *Communicating Change: how to win employee support for new business directions*, McGraw Hill (1994), ISBN 0-07-036452-4.

15 Unity Information Systems Ltd, Westpoint, 78 Queens Road, Bristol, UK. BS8 1QX. www.unity-is.com

16 *Lean Manufacturing*

Lean Manufacturing and Lean Thinking were developed in the automotive sector, influenced by Japanese practice. The principles were developed for repetitive mass-production processes. The particular principles that are applicable to 'Lean Change Management' are the concept of 'value' – what are we trying to do? (or 'intention'); and the idea of 'value stream' (making sure that everything we do creates value and there is no wasted effort). See, for example: James P. Womack and Daniel T. Jones, *Lean Thinking: Banish Waste and Create Wealth in Your Corporation*, Free Press; new edition (2003), ISBN 978-0-743-23164-0. There are also numerous web-based articles on Lean Manufacturing and Lean Thinking. I first saw the concept of 'Lean Change' in an article by Ben Jeffs, a consultant and interim manager. See his website: www.TiDi.com (Ben.Jeffs@TiDi.com)

CHAPTER 5: GET INTO ACTION

17 One of over 7,000 'Grooks' written by Danish poet, artist and scientist Piet Hein. Copyright © Piet Hein Grooks: 'The Gift'. Reprinted with kind permission from Piet Hein a/s, DK – 5500 Middelfart, Denmark. From *Grooks V Mist and Moonshine.* First English edition 1973, Borgans Forlag, Copenhagen, Denmark. ISBN 0-631-15080.

18 Paul Rogers and Marcia Blenko, 'Who has the D?' in *Harvard Business Review*, January 2006, p. 54. The authors are both partners at Bain: paul.rogers@bain.com.

19 *Five Frogs on a Log*, p. 36. See note 12 above.

20 Raymond Chandler, Letter to Alex Barris, 18 March 1949, from Dorothy Gardiner and Kathrine Sorley Walker (eds), *Raymond Chandler Speaking*, University of California Press (1997), p. 79. © 1962 The Helga Greene Literary Agency.

21 Intelligent Consulting, www.intelligent-consulting.com, Clifton Down House, 54a Whiteladies Road, Bristol, UK, BS8 2NH.

22 Theodore Roosevelt's 'Citizenship in a Republic' speech at the Sorbonne, Paris, 23 April 1910.

CHAPTER 6: BE AWARE

23 Max Born, *The Restless Universe* (2nd edition), Dover Publications (1936). Translated by Winifred M. Deans. See p. 165, in the chapter on wave mechanics.

24 *The effect of your action is unpredictable*

Patricia Shaw, *Changing Conversations in Organisations – a complexity approach to change*, Routledge (2002, reprinted 2003), p. 171. Patricia Shaw's book describes how the effects of our actions are intrinsically unpredictable. She considers the 'inherent paradox' of our participative interaction with the world: we act in 'plays that we are spontaneously forming and which are forming us at the same time'.

25 *The five-stage process*

The process described here is a variant of the more rigorous 'Plan–Do–Review' process and other derivatives of the Deming Cycle of 'Plan–Do–Check–Act'. See M. Walton and W. E. Deming, *The Deming Management Method*, New York, Dodd (1986). The Deming Cycle is summarised in Key Management Models – see note 4 above.

26 *Make awareness part of the action*

W. Timothy Gallwey, *The Inner Game of Tennis*, Pan MacMillan Ltd (1975), ISBN 978-0-330-29513-0. The book describes the importance of maintaining awareness in action, and the mental disciplines needed to do this.

27 *What's happening? What's next?*

This constant attention to the present is a skill cultivated by professional improvisers. Keith Johnstone describes this and other skills for dealing with the unexpected in his book *Impro – Improvisation and the Theatre*, Methuen Publishing Company Ltd (1981), reprinted 1989, ISBN 0-413-46430-X.

28 *Sheryl Nixon and cost reduction in the department*

Sheryl Nixon is an independent consultant who specialises in transformation programmes to improve the efficiency and effectiveness of IT. Sheryl.Nixon@btconnect.com

29 *Dialogue and the art of thinking together*

For an exploration of the nature of dialogue, see William Isaacs, *Dialogue and the Art of*

Thinking Together, Doubleday (1999), ISBN 0-385-47999-9; and David Bohm, *On Dialogue*, Routledge (1996), ISBN 0-415-14912-6.

These two books explore the skills and paradoxes involved in speaking and listening at the same time, and how this practice is important for innovation and change.

CHAPTER 7: CONTINUE

30 © Ashleigh Brilliant. Ashleigh Brilliant publishes inspirational one-liners called 'pot-shots'. He says that he is history's only full-time, professional published epigrammist. His website, www.ashleighbrilliant.com, contains hundreds of epigrams and sayings. I first bought his postcards from hippy shops in the dilapidated Bristol docks of the 1970s. So he's been going quite a while.

31 Encourage traditions, conventions and behaviours which reinforce the change

I first heard this definition of 'culture' from Carolyn Taylor. The idea that 'culture is about messages' is expanded in her book *Walking the Talk – building a culture for success*, Random House Business Books (2005), ISBN 1-8441-3807-0.

32 The classic model of business change describes planned progress towards a fixed goal

Classic models are, for example, PRINCE2 and MSP (Managing Successful Programmes). The OGC website (Office of Government Computing) describes these.

A book review entitled 'Be firm, be flexible' in *The Economist* of 12 July 2007 notes that 'Strategy today still assumes that corporate decision-makers are like generals on the battlefield, fighting in a sequential world where one step is "then" followed by another along a route clearly marked "either/or".' The reviewer notes the current dilemma between the steadfast progress towards fixed goals and a more flexible approach.

33 Securing the future

Somerfield is a UK supermarket chain (www.somerfield.com).

CHAPTER 8: CONVERSATIONS THAT WORK

34 Conversation is a skill

Theodore Zeldin, *Conversation: How talk can change our lives*, Harvill Press (1998), ISBN 1-86046-662-1.

Professor Zeldin advocates the enjoyment and development of conversational skills. This is a tiny book, illustrated with his idiosyncratic watercolours.

CHAPTER 9: MEETINGS WHERE CHANGE HAPPENS

35 Examples of meetings where change happens: Work Out

'Work Out' is a process in which a structured meeting is used to bring about specific types of change. See, for example, Dave Ulrich, Steve Kerr and Ron Ashkenas, *The GE Work Out – how to implement GE's revolutionary method for busting bureaucracy and attacking organisational problems – fast!*, McGraw Hill (2002), ISBN 0-07-138416-2.

Also see my article at www.JaneNorthcote.com: 'Work Out: Finding and implementing "quick hits" to improve productivity immediately'.

CONCLUSION

36 Eyvind H. Wichmann, *Berkeley Physics Course, Vol. 4 'Quantum Physics'*, McGraw Hill College (1968).

FOR FURTHER READING

Communicating Change by T. J. Larkin and Sandar Larkin (see note 14 above) is a wonderfully clear book that gives provocative advice on how to communicate with people during major change programmes. The authors point out common pitfalls with staff surveys and have views on how to improve them. They clearly link intention and action, and give startling examples of what happens when intentions are not properly communicated.

INDEX

7-S model 140

action
  characteristics of 57–60
  choosing most direct 66–9
  choosing most effective 64–6, 69
  distinction from activity 60–64, 69
Action Lab
  as example of a meeting 124
  direct action principle 68–9
activity, distinction from action 60–64, 69
anticipation, as self-motivation 76
Appreciative Inquiry 141
Ashkenas, Ron, *The GE Work Out* 144
attentiveness, importance of 85–6
attractors, as self-motivation 78
awareness
  attentiveness 85–6
  being connected 91–3
  getting feedback 87–9
  practical application 93

Ball, Philip, *Critical Mass - how one thing leads to another* 141
Band-aid 76
Berkeley Physics Course (Wichmann) 133, 145
Blenko, Marcia 73
  'Who has the D?' 143
Bohm, David, *On Dialogue* 144
Born, Max, *The Restless Universe* 85, 143
boundaries, and creativity 50–51
Brilliant, Ashleigh 100, 144
budgeting processes 101
Business System Diamond 140

Champy, James, *Reengineering the Corporation: A Manifesto for Business Revolution* 140
Chandler, Raymond 79, 143
change, definition 9
changes, small and big 9
Changing Conversations in Organisations (Shaw) 85, 143
'Citizenship in a Republic' (Roosevelt) 143
Co-active Coaching (Whitworth, Kimsey-House and Sandhal) 141
commitment, as self-motivation 77
Communicating Change: how to win employee support for new business directions (Larkin and Larkin) 142, 145
communication
  two-way 102
  see also awareness; intentions, stating, listening
Complexity and Management (Stacey, Griffin and Shaw) 141
continuing change
  embedding change 99, 100–102
  what next 97–100
  continuity 52–3
Conversation: How talk can change our lives (Zeldin) 144
conversations
  hearing 'No' 115–16
  that don't drive action 117–18
  to drive action 118
  types 111–13
  what doesn't work 116–18
  what works 113–14
corporate processes, embedding change 101

Corporate Strategy (Lynch) 140
'Creativity is not Enough' (Levitt) 140
Critical Mass - how one thing leads to another (Ball) 141
culture 102, 144

Define–Measure–Analyse–Improve–Control (DMAIC) 140
The Deming Management Method (Walton and Deming) 143
Dialogue and the art of thinking together (Isaacs) 91, 143–4
direct action, choosing 66–9
DMAIC (Define–Measure–Analyse–Improve–Control) 140
do it
 see self-motivation, get yourself to do things
Dot Charts 127–8

effective action, choosing 64–6, 69
embedding change 99, 100–102
emergent order 141
enlarging change 99
extending change 99

Feldman, Mark L., *Five Frogs on a Log – A CEO's Guide to Accelerating the Transition in Mergers, Acquisitions, and Gut Wrenching Change* 142–3
Fischer, Rolf (proprietor, Hôtel Jean-Jacques Rousseau, Geneva) 65–6
Five Frogs on a Log – A CEO's Guide to Accelerating the Transition in Mergers, Acquisitions, and Gut Wrenching Change (Feldman and Spratt) 142–3
'from' and 'to'
 articulating 31–9
 setting boundaries 50–51
 SMART objectives 40–45, 141
 what stays the same 46–50, 51–3

Gallwey, W. Timothy, *The Inner Game of Tennis* (Gallwey) 143
Gardiner, Dorothy, *Raymond Chandler Speaking* 143
The GE Work Out (Ulrich, Kerr and Ashkenas) 144
generalising change 99
The Gift (poem, Hein) 73, 142
Gioja, Linda, *Surfing the Edge of Chaos* 141
goals, changing 103–105, 107
Griffin, Douglas, Complexity and Management 141
Grooks V Mist and Moonshine (Hein) 142

Hammer, Michael, *Reengineering the Corporation: A Manifesto for Business Revolution* 140
Hammond, Sue Annis, *The Thin Book of Appreciative Inquiry* 141
The Heart of Change (Kotter) 141
Hein, Piet, *The Gift* 73, 142
help, asking for 77
Holpp, Larry, *What is Six Sigma?* 140
Hôtel Jean-Jacques Rousseau, Geneva 142
 see also stories, Rolf's hotel

Id's Hospit (Pugh) 140
Impro – Improvisation and the Theatre (Johnstone) 143
The Inner Game of Tennis (Gallwey) 143
Intelligent Consulting 80, 143
intentions
 changing 103–106
 definitions 13, 16–17
 examples of 14–15
 misunderstandings 22–5
 restating for self-motivation 75
 revealed by actions 20–21
 stating 17–20, 26, 106–107
 see also awareness, getting feedback
intervals in meetings 129
Isaacs, William, *Dialogue and the art of thinking together* 91, 143–4

Jeffs, Ben 142
Johnstone, Keith, *Impro – Improvisation and the Theatre* 143
Jones, Daniel T., *Lean Thinking: Banish Waste and Create Wealth in Your Corporation* 142
Kaufmann; 'Ulrich Kaufmann' story 46, 53
Kerr, Steve, *The GE Work Out* 144
Key Management Models (ten Have et al.) 140

Kimsey-House, Henry, *Co-active Coaching* 141
Kotter, John
The Heart of Change 141
Leading Change 140–41

Larkin, Sandar, and Larkin, T. J.,
Communicating Change, how to win employee support for new business directions 142, 145
Leading Change (Kotter) 140–41
Lean Change Management 142
Lean Manufacturing 68, 142
Lean Thinking 68, 142
Lean Thinking: Banish Waste and Create Wealth in Your Corporation (Womack and Jones) 142
Levitt, Theodore, 'Creativity is not Enough' 140
listening
to measure effects of action 91
while in action 86
see also awareness; conversations; *On Dialogue*
Lynch, Richard, *Corporate Strategy* 140

making change happen 8–9
Managing Successful Programmes (MSP) 144
measurement phase 86–7
meetings
change rather than action lists 123–4
making change happen 126–9, 137
method, step-by-step
alternatives 140
overview 5, 135
'Mike' story 60–61, 114
Milleman, Mark, *Surfing the Edge of Chaos* 141
models of change 103, 133

Nixon, Sheryl (consultant) 89–91, 143

'Omar' story 97–102
On Dialogue (Bohm) 144
other people, as self-motivation 77

Pande, Pete, *What is Six Sigma?* 140
Pascale, Richard T., *Surfing the Edge of Chaos* 141
performance management processes 101
'Philip Marlowe' 79
Phillipps, Nigel
(MD, Unity Information Systems) 67–8, 105–106
planning, limiting 86
Pol-Coyne, Fiona, *Key Management Models* 140
Pot-Shots 100, 144
pragmatism 133
preparation for action 60–61
PRINCE2 9, 144
progress measuring in meetings 127–8
Pugh, Sheenagh,
What If This Road vi (frontispiece), 140

Raymond Chandler Speaking (Gardiner and Sorley Walker) 143
Reengineering the Corporation: A Manifesto for Business Revolution (Hammer and Champy) 140
reframing change 99, 103–106
repeating change 99
requests 114–16
restating intentions 106–107
The Restless Universe (Born) 85, 143
Rogers, Paul 73
'Who has the D?' 143
Roosevelt, Theodore 81, 143

Sanderson Recruitment *see* Walrond, Nick
Sandhal, Phil, *Co-active Coaching* 141
scope, of change 35
self-motivation
find an attractor 78
get yourself to do things 74, 81
remove choice 78
use other people 77
use your mind 75–6
self-organising systems 141
Shaw, Patricia
Changing Conversations in Organisations 85, 143
Complexity and Management 141

Six Sigma process 140
SMART objectives 40–45, 141
Somerfield 105–106, 144
Sorley Walker, Kathrine, *Raymond Chandler Speaking* 143
Spratt, Michael F.,
Five Frogs on a Log – A CEO's Guide to Accelerating the Transition in Mergers, Acquisitions, and Gut Wrenching Change 142–3
St Clement Danes 142
St Clement, Eastcheap 142
Stacey, Ralph, *Complexity and Management* 141
status quo
- activities maintaining as distinct from action 64–6
- and change programmes 32
- changing corporate processes 101
- in measurement phase 86
- keeping aspects of
  see 'from' and 'to', what stays the same

Stevens, Frans, *Key Management Models* 140
stories
- changing business processes in a distillery 19–20
- cost reduction in the department 90–91
- the Manager's Away Day 21
- Nick Walrond improves Account Management 41
- Nick Walrond assesses the impact of change 92–3
- Nick Walrond gets into action: selling a new product to customers 79–80
- Nigel Phillipps takes direct action 67–8
- Project Initiation Panel 124–5
- Rolf Fischer's hotel 65–6
- Sanderson's Delivery Team Stays the Same 52
- saving time in a bank branch 50–51
- Securing the future, Nigel and Unity 105–106
- a story about pricing 33–4
- telephone conference 22–5
- the 'Ulrich Kaufmann' story, maintaining the status quo 46, 53

support for action 61–4
Surfing the Edge of Chaos (Pascale, Milleman and Gioja) 141

Taylor, Carolyn, *Walking the Talk – building a culture for success* 144
ten Have, Steven, and Wouter, *Key Management Models* 140
The Thin Book of Appreciative Inquiry (Hammond) 141
trapping yourself 78

Ulrich, Dave, *The GE Work Out* 144
Unity Information Systems 142
see also Phillipps, Nigel

Value Driver Analysis 142
Van der Elst, Marcel, *Key Management Models* 140
vision 16, 141

Walking the Talk – building a culture for success (Taylor) 144
Walrond, Nick (MD, Sanderson Recruitment) 41, 52, 79–80, 92–3
Walton, M., The Deming Management Method 143
What If This Road (Pugh) vi (frontispiece), 140
What is Six Sigma? (Pande and Holpp) 140
Whitworth, Laura, *Co-active Coaching* 141
'Who has the D?' (Rogers and Blenko) 143
Wichmann, Eyvind H., *Berkeley Physics Course* 133, 145
Womack, James P., *Lean Thinking: Banish Waste and Create Wealth in Your Corporation* 142
Work Out 144

Zeldin, Theodore, *Conversation: How talk can change our lives* 144

ACKNOWLEDGEMENTS

Many people have helped me write this book, and I am grateful to all of them.

Some deserve a special mention. For wise, honest and articulate suggestions on early drafts I am indebted to Paul Turton and Robert Smithbury. Nick Walrond, Nigel Phillipps, Sheryl Nixon and Rolf Fischer generously answered my questions and contributed their stories. There are many others, clients and friends, who have shown me the way.

Throughout this project I have relied on the organisational skills of Sonja Jefferson, and the text has been vastly improved by her perceptive observations. Lizzie Everard's designs have been a continual source of inspiration.

The Barbican Public Library, the City Business Library, the King's College London Maughan Library and the Kipferl Austrian Café on Long Lane, London EC2, were wonderful, calm places for thinking.

These people and places made this book possible. Thanks to all.